FIGHTERS AGAINST FASCISM

FIGHTERS AGAINST FASCISM

British heroes of the Spanish Civil War

MAX ARTHUR

Collins

This paperback edition
published in 2010

First published in 2009 by Collins
A division of HarperCollins Publishers
77–85 Fulham Palace Road
London W6 8JB
www.collins.co.uk

1

Max Arthur asserts the moral right to be
identified as the author of this work

A catalogue record for this book is
available from the British Library

ISBN 978-0-00-733080-5

Set in Linotype Giovanni by
Rowland Phototypesetting Ltd, Bury St Edmunds, Suffolk
Printed and bound in Great Britain by Clays Ltd, St Ives plc

Mixed Sources
Product group from well-managed
forests and other controlled sources
www.fsc.org Cert no. SW-COC-1806
© 1996 Forest Stewardship Council

FSC is a non-profit international organisation established to promote the
responsible management of the world's forests. Products carrying the FSC
label are independently certified to assure consumers that they come
from forests that are managed to meet the social, economic and
ecological needs of present and future generations.

Find out more about HarperCollins and the environment at
www.harpercollins.co.uk/green

This book is dedicated to the 2,500 British and Irish volunteers who fought alongside the Spanish people in their heroic struggle against Fascism from 1936 to 1939. And, in particular, to the 526 who lost their lives.

CONTENTS

ACKNOWLEDGEMENTS

At Collins, I would like to thank my editor Louise Stanley for her skill, tenacity and patience. Also Charlotte Allibone and Katherine Patrick for marketing and publicity, and everyone else who helped bring the book to fruition.

Marlene Sidaway, the Secretary of the International Brigade Memorial Trust, introduced me to all the veterans and has been a remarkable source of encouragement for both the book and documentary. Marlene, who cares profoundly for the welfare of the last surviving veterans, organised an emotional trip for four of them, and their families and carers, to Spain in October 2008 for the 70th anniversary celebrations. I am totally indebted to her.

Vicky Thomas underwent a considerable task in transcribing all the tapes of the interviews, and produced copy that was a joy for me to edit. I am, as always, profoundly grateful to her.

Matt Richards filmed each of the veterans and did so with consummate skill. He superbly directed the two-part documentary that accompanies the book, *The Brits Who Fought for Spain*, which was produced by Tris Payne for the History Channel.

I am most grateful for the encouragement of Professor Paul Preston of the London School of Economics, the foremost expert on the Spanish Civil War.

I was ably supported by my dear friends Sir Martin and Lady Gilbert, Don and Liz McClen, David and Annie Rickards and Susan Jeffrey. Ruth Cowen, as she always has, provided care, advice, humour and affection. My final thanks are to Lucia Corti, just for being Lucia.

Bay of Biscay

El Ferrol
La Coruña
Gijón Santander
Guernica San Sebastián
F R A N C E

Oviedo
Bilbao
*frontier closed by France
to Republican refugees, 1938*

GALICIA
ASTURIAS
Santiago
de Compostela
BASQUE PROVINCES
León
NAVARRE
Pamplona
Ebro
Vigo
Burgos
*Nationalist
Government H.Q.*
Zaragoza
CATALONIA

LEÓN
Valladolid
A
R
A
G
O
N
Belchite
Barcelona

Oporto
Salamanca
Tarragona

PORTUGAL
*besieged by Nationalists;
occupied on 28 March 1939*
Guadalajara
Madrid
Teruel

Tagus
Brunete
Jarama
Castellón
de la Plana

Cáceres
S P A I N
Toledo
Valencia

Lisbon
Mérida
EXTREMADURA
C A S T I L E
Albacete
International Brigade base
Majorca
Mahón
Palma

Badajoz
Lopera
MURCIA
Ibiza
Alicante

Huelva
Córdoba
Cartagena

Seville
Granada
Almería

Cádiz
Málaga

Ceuta
Gibraltar
(British)
Mediterranean
Sea

Tangier
SPANISH MOROCCO
ALGERIA

*Atlantic
Ocean*

The Spanish Civil War,
1936–39

○ 'International Brigade' operations

← main Nationalist attacks

← main Republican attacks

Nationalist, July 1936

Nationalist, October 1937

Nationalist, July 1938

Nationalist, February 1939

Republican, March 1939

PREFACE

The Real Band of Brothers stems from a chance meeting with the actor Alison Steadman in 2003 at the launch of my book *Forgotten Voices of the Great War*, where she read the moving words of Kitty Eckersley, whose husband had died on the Western Front. I met Alison again five years later and she introduced me to her friend, Marlene Sidaway, also an actor. Marlene lived for many years with David Marshall, one of the earliest British volunteers in the International Brigades, and was also the Secretary of the International Brigade Memorial Trust. In this role, she told me, she was in close touch with the last British survivors of the Brigade – and, from that meeting, the book began to take shape.

To many people in the UK today, the Spanish Civil War remains something of a grey area – a conflict in which British troops were not engaged, and one that was eclipsed in the public perception by the Second World War. But the Spanish Civil War was a vicious and prolonged battle, the repercussions of which still reverberate through that country today. Many towns were destroyed and their populations massacred; the lives of half a million men, women and children were lost. Furthermore, while the British Government did not support the democratically elected Republican regime in Spain, individuals from the UK and other nations across Europe, incensed by the injustice of the Spanish struggle, volunteered their services to fight for democracy.

In July 1936, the army generals including General Franco led a savage military coup to depose Spain's elected government – a left-wing coalition of the Spanish Socialist Workers' Party (PSOE), the Republican left, the Communists and various regional nationalist groups. This Fascist aggression was not isolated in Spain; in the early 1930s, extreme right-wing movements were also growing under Mussolini in Italy, Hitler in Germany and, to the alarm of left-wing parties there, under Oswald Mosley in Britain.

Supported by his Blackshirts, Mosley tried to impose his authoritarian philosophies on the working-class population of London's East End, and his political meetings often ended in violence. Eventually, in a well-orchestrated show of strength, groups of trade unionists, Communists and Jews joined forces to denounce Mosley's racist ideology and prevent his jackbooted thugs from marching through their streets – it was a stand-off that became known as the infamous Battle of Cable Street.

Some of the men and women who had seen off Mosley on that fateful day later volunteered to fight in Spain in what became known as the International Brigades. Much to the fury of these volunteers, the British Government of the day had adopted a policy of non-intervention. Not only would there be no British military support for the Spanish against Franco's forces, there would be no official medical or material aid either. Although news from the Spanish war was sparse in any but the left-wing press, a growing number of people travelled to London to sign up with the Communist Party, and, in defiance of French laws against partisan military groups, made their way across the Channel, through France and over the Pyrenees to support the Spanish Republican army. Some were motivated by their political beliefs; others by their horror at the humanitarian catastrophe unfolding in Spain. The working people, already poor and living from hand to mouth, were facing starvation and disease, and many British doctors and nurses set out for Spain to offer their skills in order to alleviate the suffering their consciences could not ignore.

In the three-year conflict – which has been dubbed the first battle of the Second World War – many of those volunteers lost their lives. To all who freely offered their services, for whom the cause was indeed just and one they were prepared to die for, the war was a life-changing experience – and one that none would regret, despite the consequences.

As I started working on *The Real Band of Brothers*, just eight veterans of the International Brigades remained in Britain and, together with the award-winning documentary maker

Matt Richards, I travelled across the country to interview and film these remarkable characters. The oldest, Lou Kenton, turned 100 in September 2008, and former nurse Penny Feiwel's hundredth birthday is in April 2009. She is still full of vigour – and still cursing Franco for inflicting the terrible injuries on innocent children that she witnessed. Archaeology student Sam Lesser fought for two years to hold the City University of Madrid. Paddy Cochrane, who at seven had seen his father shot by the Black and Tans in Dublin, believed that he himself would suffer a violent death in Spain. Bob Doyle, who, after being held prisoner by the Fascists, returned years later to stamp and swear on Franco's grave. Jack Jones would later become leader of the Transport and General Workers' Union, and fought fearlessly at the Ebro in the last battle of the war. Les Gibson, a founder of the Young Communist League in west London, fought through Jarama, Brunete and the Ebro, and survived life-threatening colitis to return to the action. Jack Edwards, at home a very active union member and political activist, returned from the war with his determination to fight Fascism undiminished; within months he joined the RAF to continue the battle against Hitler.

Over a number of weeks I had the great pleasure of interviewing these eight extraordinary survivors in their own homes. Matt Richards recorded their testimonies on film and tape, and has subsequently written a script based on the interviews, which was commissioned as a two-part documentary for the History Channel – *The Brits Who Fought for Spain*.

All these old 'Brigaders' had endured an extremely tough Edwardian childhood, but retained an extraordinary vitality and a clear perspective on how the war had changed their lives forever. I am in awe of their still-vibrant sense of anger and defiance. Since writing the original preface Jack Jones and Bob Doyle, both indomitable spirits, have died. I was privileged to have been at Bob's bedside the day before he died.

Some had told their story before, but others were opening up after a lifetime in which they had avoided talking about the war. Their testimonies are in their own words but allowance must be made for the age and frailty of their memories. Wherever possible I have checked the historical details, but sometimes the facts are buried in time. Bob Doyle and Jack Jones kindly gave me permission to use additional extracts from their respective books, *Brigadista* and *Union Man*.

It is now 70 years since the end of the Spanish Civil War, in which over 500 of the 2,500 British volunteers for the International Brigades were killed. All the survivors, however, were united in the one belief – that they were fighting against the evil of Fascism, and that it was no less than their duty to do their bit. As more than one speculated, if other European governments had supported the Spanish Republic and quashed the Fascist threat in its infancy, the course of history might have been different, and perhaps there would even have been no Second World War.

Whatever their sense of the role of the Spanish Civil War in a historical context, all are personally bound by the values of comradeship and deep loyalty. They fought for a cause, asked for no payment, and saw many friends die. But every one agreed that they would do it all again.

These are their words – I have been but a catalyst.

Max Arthur

London

January 2009

Words etched on the memorial to the
International Brigades on London's South Bank

'They went because their open eyes
could see no other way'
C. Day Lewis

'Yet Freedom! Yet thy banner, torn, but flying, streams
like the thunderstorm AGAINST the wind'
Byron

LOU KENTON

Born 1 September 1908 in Stepney, east London

I was born in a block of flats – a tenement – in the East End, in Stepney, in Adler Street, which doesn't exist any more. I had eight brothers altogether, but some died. I was the first one to be born in England (my family was originally from Ukraine). My father died of TB when I was fourteen – he was working in a sweatshop for a tailor. I missed my bar mitzvah because he'd just died.

I joined the Communist Party in 1929, because it was the only party that was fighting Fascism. I met my first wife, who came from Austria, and together we were both in the Communist Party, although she wasn't very active – she was a masseuse and spent her lifetime working.

We all had a political dislike for the Fascists. Mosley was the leader of the Fascists in Britain and he was anti-Labour – and anti-Communist, of course – and we often had fights when they tried to break up our meetings – and we did the same to them. We hated Mosley and there were always battles going on in the East End. The headquarters of the Fascists were in Bethnal Green, and we, the Communist Party, were mostly in Stepney.

At that time London was a much-divided place – in the east there were lots of trade unions, factories and the tailoring was mostly Communist. The first big encounter was when Mosley announced that he was going to march through the East End of London on 4 October 1936. His main slogan was 'down with the Jews'. We had enough notice to run a campaign against the march. Until then Mosley had had setbacks, but was going from strength to strength. The point we tried to bring to public attention was that this was not just a provocation of the Jews: this march was an attack on the people of Britain as a whole. We tried to win the support of all sections of the population, which indeed we did. Not only the local trade council, but trade union branches from all over London and other parts of the country, supported the campaign to stop Mosley marching through east London. Of course, the Jewish population was on our side, although the official view of the Jewish Board of Deputies was 'Don't make trouble – just be quiet'. But we were able to get the majority of the Jewish population of east London on our side, as well as the dockers – they were the main big sections. Every grouping also had a job to do in the organisation of the whole of what has now become known as the Battle of Cable Street. My job was to organise my own Party branch of Holborn, which included the print workers, to occupy the ground around Aldgate Station. Mosley was going to march from the Minories (around Tower Hill), where he had assembled with the help of the police, through Aldgate, along Whitechapel Road, into Bethnal Green, where he had a certain amount of support. I had two jobs, firstly for my branch to be the first line of defence in Aldgate. What we were supposed to do I don't know – there were only about thirty or forty of us and we didn't know how big the crowd would be. We imagined that we would hold the Mosley crowd for even a few minutes, while the rest of the crowd would rally. In the event, the crowd was great: it stretched right along the Whitechapel Road, Commercial Road, Gardiner's Corner, right up towards Aldgate Station itself. The crowd was so thick that you couldn't move. There were a number of trams in the area and they were stuck in the middle of the crowd. You can imagine the sight – something like half a million people with these trams stuck all over the place. Of course, the word got to Mosley, and to the police, that they couldn't possibly go through Aldgate.

They tried to redirect the march the other way, down Leman Street from the Minories into Cable Street, making a detour of Whitechapel Road. I had a motorbike at the time and was able to whizz around the periphery of the crowd, going from section to section to warn them what was going on. We had a number of people watching the Fascists and quickly telling the crowd what was happening. We were able to get word to the majority of the crowd in Commercial Road, which was some way from Cable Street, of what was happening. The dockers themselves were manning Cable Street and had thrown up barricades. As soon as the word got around that Mosley was on the way towards Cable Street, within minutes thousands of people were there. Although hundreds of police and the Mosley crowd tried to break through, they were stopped. Mosley then had to go back to the Minories and finally the police chief said there was no possibility of them going through the East End. They turned round and went the other way, towards the City, to the Embankment, and dispersed. That was really the great Battle of Cable Street: a major historic event and the first real defeat of Mosley.

Can you imagine the celebration throughout the East End that day? People were dancing in the streets, hugging each other. They had defeated Mosley – defeated Fascism. And although people had not yet fully realised what Fascism was, they could see what the Fascists' intentions were.

I was married to Lilian at the time and we were living in Holborn and we were both very active. I was in Holborn at the beginning of the Spanish Civil War and the branch, being more or less in the centre of London, helped to steward the big meetings taking place in Conway Hall, Farringdon Hall and Kingsway Hall. Appeals were made for money, food and support – they were very enthusiastic meetings.

I remember clearly, when the revolt started, how immediately the whole of the left-wing movement rallied in support of Spain. The majority of the people, however, didn't take much interest and a good many were influenced by the press of the time, which condemned it as a Bolshevik, anti-Christian revolution. On our side we got to know early on about the real issues in Spain. The formation of the International Brigades gave it a personal interest, as people we knew began to make their way there. Very quickly we began to know the background to the Spanish struggle and the campaign in support of the Spanish Government grew in strength. Soon after the start of the civil war, Mussolini and Hitler sent Italian and German armies and air force over to help Franco. The Spanish Government, the legitimate government of the day, tried to buy arms. Britain and France were able to win the support of the League of Nations on a policy of so-called 'non-intervention'. The reality of non-intervention meant that the Spanish Government was unable to buy arms, while the Fascists were free to buy what they wanted. The Spaniards were only able to get arms from Russia in a limited quantity, and from Mexico. Right through the war the army of the Spanish Government was far worse equipped than the Fascist side.

In Britain the movement grew in a number of ways. An organisation called British Medical Aid had been set up to raise money for ambulances. Very soon they opened first one and then another hospital in Spain. British doctors and nurses went to service these and other front-line hospitals. There was a great campaign to raise money and whole lorry-loads of food were sent. There were also the youth food ships for Spain, which brought regular supplies. The British navy blockaded the coast and tried to stop the food ships, but several got through the blockade. Then, very soon, the refugees from the Basque country came over – we had several hundred Basque children in Britain who were looked after mostly in and around London. I think hardly a week went by without demonstrations and meetings taking place. Gradually the movement grew and became a very powerful crusade.

While this was happening individuals were going to Spain, isolated from each other, and joining one of the Republican units when they got there. Then the call went out throughout the whole world for volunteers to form the International Brigades.

One evening myself and Lilian and my dear friend Ben Glazer walked along the Embankment. We walked – stopped at many coffee stalls – talking, wondering what it would be like in Spain. We didn't finally decide until we reached a coffee stall at Westminster Bridge, opposite the House of Commons. I think we had already decided to go, but didn't say so in as many words. I think we were deeply fearful in our hearts, but none of us wanted to show our fears. What would it be like? Would we ever come back? What if we were captured? And when we decided – how we embraced! Lilian kissed us both. We linked arms and walked almost cheerfully down Whitehall to the all-night Lyons Corner House just off Trafalgar Square for more coffee and eggs and bacon. From there we decided that tomorrow morning we would go and volunteer.

Lilian and Ben both went off the next day. It was the last time I was to see Ben.

I was accepted, but the Party asked me to hold fire for three or four weeks while I cleared up the work that I was involved in as secretary. When I got to work next day I handed in my notice, and the Father of Chapel in charge of the print said, 'What do you think you're doing? You can't just walk out, jobs are very precious.' But I said, 'I'm going to Spain.' In those days an apprenticeship was so important – if you got a job you'd got it for life.

While Lilian went with the British Medical Aid Committee, Ben and the others had to make their own way to Paris, then through the Pyrenees. If you went through the British Medical Aid you could get your passport and the visa for Spain – but you also had to sign a document at the Foreign Office saying that if you were in trouble you wouldn't call on the British Ambassador. That was fine. Lilian and I sold our home and gave our stuff away. I went to live in a room with Phil Piratin in east London, pending the time when I was ready to go. When I went along, blow me, they had changed the arrangements and they no longer, at least at that particular time, accepted anybody without military experience.

What to do? I went to the British Medical Aid and they said, 'Yes, we will have you, if you can drive a lorry and service it.' Again, what to do? So I went along to a garage in Walworth Road, offered my services free if I could be taught how to change wheels, change tyres, drive a lorry, etc. I went every evening after work and worked there for seven or eight hours. After about three or four weeks I felt competent enough to drive a lorry, went back to the Medical Aid and said I was ready to go on my motorbike but could also drive an ambulance or a lorry. I went off three or four days later.

My mother knew that Lilian had gone and kept asking, 'Are you going?' and 'Must you go?' and all the things a mother would say. I was anxious not to upset her, and, in the clumsy way most young people deal with these matters, I said that, if she was going to cry every time I came round before leaving, I wouldn't come again – just go off. An awful thing to say!

I asked a friend to be present when I said goodbye. There was I, all packed, equipped with a new pair of leather leggings, leather gloves, leather jacket – which I had never had before. I kissed my mother goodbye, turned around the top of the road and waved. Later I was told she didn't cry until I had gone, and then she broke down.

Came the day when I was going, word got round. I belonged to a club, the YCL (Young Communist League), and some dockers all came to the top of the street, Adler Street, between Whitechapel and Commercial Road, to see me off. There must have been several hundred, because I was still one of the first. I got on my bike, waved to them and started off. You won't believe this: I didn't have a map. I had no idea which way to go. All I knew was to get to the Elephant and Castle and head for Dover. I had my passport, visa and signed documents from the Foreign Office and knew I had to make my way to Barcelona. I can't remember how I ever got there. I vaguely remember going right across France, making my way to the south.

I used to sleep by the roadside every night – I didn't have money for lodgings. I had to get to Perpignan [to enter Spain] and how on earth I got there I don't know. I had just a little money the crowd in London had collected for me so I could eat on the road. When I got to Perpignan I thought, 'at last, Spain'. I looked and I couldn't see any signs but I saw a crowd of workers having a cup of tea in a café. I went up to them and asked which was the way to Spain. They couldn't speak English and I couldn't speak Spanish, so I said, 'Me, Spain, "Boom Boom!".' So when they stopped laughing they gathered round me, gave me a meal, and showed me the road to España, the first time I'd ever seen the sign for España.

My first real recollection of Spain was arriving at a great castle at Figueres – an enormous place – and outside the gates were two men on sentry duty. I stopped and asked them where to go. They spoke a little English and opened the gate. I rode in through this gate and the square of the castle was like a fort – as big as Trafalgar Square – hundreds if not thousands of men sitting around talking. I later learnt that was the first staging post for the people who had climbed the Pyrenees. I was the first one who had arrived on a motorbike. I think it was an American who first said to me, 'If you want to keep that bike, never leave it, even to go to the bog – because there are so many people who would like to have your bike.'

There were literally hundreds who had found their way to the castle at Figueres. They'd walked over the mountains and they had their feet seen to and were given food. Each group from the different countries gathered together. There was a group from Britain and I went and joined them, and they were very keen to see a bloke with a motorbike. Several asked me if they could travel with me on the bike, but I said no – I was going to pick my wife up.

I went to Barcelona where the offices of the Brigade were. Remembering what the American had said, I saw a policeman and tried to explain to him – though of course he didn't speak a word of English. I somehow managed to persuade him to look after my bike while I was in the office and he nodded. He straddled the bike and with his hand on his revolver he was going to shoot anybody who'd try and pinch it. I got my instructions to go to a little town called Benicasim. I slept in the office that night. The next morning I went by bike from Barcelona to the HQ in Valencia, where there was a convalescent home for the British Battalion. I didn't know at the time, but, looking back later, I realise that I had arrived in Spain at the end of the Battle of Jarama in February 1937, which was the great turning point of the war. Until then the Fascists were advancing very rapidly; they were right in front of Madrid. If Madrid had fallen in those days, less than a year after the start of the war, it would have been the end. And the call went out, 'Everything for Madrid – save Madrid'. The British Battalion had been building up and training as a unit. They hadn't yet quite had their full training, but, because of the urgency of the situation, were thrown into the front line.

I wasn't there, but I have heard stories of how they marched through Madrid. People in their thousands were ready to fight and build barricades in front of Madrid. Here, for the first time, an organised unit marched into action, and the emotion that it aroused among the people of Madrid can only be imagined.

Before I got to Valencia I found the place where wounded Brigaders were convalescing after the Battle of Jarama and that was where Lilian had been sent. It was wonderful to see her. We lost more than half of our battalion, killed and wounded, in that battle. It wasn't just a convalescent home – it was also being used as a hospital. There were a number of wounded; several nurses had been in Jarama and they told me that it was very, very serious, very tense. One nurse from the north had had a nervous breakdown and said to me, 'You mustn't come out here, young man. You should go back home. We don't stand a chance.' Another nurse who had been with her tried to calm her and said to me, 'It is tough, but you knew what you were coming to, anyway.' Very soon, those who were well enough to travel went to a proper con- valescent home which was run by British-speaking volunteers, at Benicasim. The others either went back to the front, or to one of the hospitals for further treatment. I was told to report to one of the British hospitals in a place called Valdeganga. We had two hospitals – one in Valdeganga and one in a place called Cuenca. I reported and I spent the rest of my time in Spain based in Valdeganga. I took Lilian with me on the bike.

Every day I was either on my motorcycle or driving an ambulance, picking up wounded from the base camps. Often

I would go to different units of the battalion scattered around Spain with messages or parcels of medical equipment, where they were in short supply.

We knew the Fascists were killing and murdering all the trade unionists they could find, and I had an unhappy time out there for the first few months because I was on my own, going from hospital to hospital.

Everywhere I went, my memory of the warmth and friendship of the Spanish people is still very vivid. I didn't speak any Spanish – well, very little. I could ask the way to a place, but I could never understand the answer. After a while I got into a habit that, if I came to a village, I would stop in the centre and people would look at me curiously from all around the square. After a while somebody would come and try and talk to me in Spanish, and I would explain that I was English, in the International Brigade. When they heard I was in the International Brigade, their hearts opened and I was taken in, often given food, though they had very little of it. There I first had a drink of anise – which nearly knocked my head off. This happened almost everywhere I went, in every village. From the hospital in Valdeganga I went to Madrid and several times to Barcelona, Valencia and Albacete, which was the base of the International Brigades. Generally, if I had to spend more than one night, I would stop and find the military controller of the area, and I was allowed to sleep there – but I never left my bike. I always made a point of bedding down beside the bike and resting my head on the wheel. They all thought it was very curious and very strange, but it was the only way I kept that bike. I lived on grapes growing by the roadside, for days on end.

I have one feeling of unease – whether I did the right thing or not I don't know. On one occasion when I was at Albacete I met Wally Tapsall, who was the political commissar of the battalion, and Fred Copeman, who was a commander. When they saw me with the bike, they said, 'Hey, we want you in the battalion – we could use you.'

I said, 'OK – by all means. You just get in touch with the hospital.'

They said, 'Oh no, it would take too long. You just come along and we will straighten it out later.'

I said I wasn't prepared to do that, because I was attached to the hospital. I often wonder whether I did right. It is one of those things – you never know.

I remember when Harry Pollitt, who was the General Secretary of the Communist Party of Great Britain, came to speak to the battalion. He took a number of the wounded and members of the staff to hear him. It was a wonderful experience, because Harry was a well-known speaker. He had the art of speaking about what you felt in your own heart and on this occasion he spoke with such pride of the men who were there and pride in the fact that it was the Communist Party that inspired the formation of the Brigade.

I used to go to the village every day where the bakery woman had a young child of about ten or eleven, and she took to me. She would wait for my lorry to arrive, she would take me by the hand, lead me into the bakery and always insisted that I had something to eat or drink. Occasionally I would take her and her mother for a trip into the nearest town or to the hospital, and she loved it. Sometimes she would get all her friends to come for a trip on the lorry.

Occasionally in the hospital things were quiet, and then an ambulance would arrive with either wounded or people who had come from other hospitals for convalescence. Everybody would jump to action. The whole place was a hive of activity, getting their beds ready, looking after them, helping them to wash, finding new clothes for them, feeding them.

I don't know how long I had been there before I had heard that Ben Glazer, my friend who went to Spain three or four weeks ahead of me, had been killed. Somehow I accepted it. Every time we heard of a friend or somebody in the Brigade who had been killed, somebody who we knew either by name or personally, there was never any – I won't say sadness – but there wasn't any great shock – almost as though we had always expected it. Looking back on my own feelings when I came to Spain, it was almost as though I was saying goodbye – almost as though I was expecting to be killed. After Jarama, and then later the Ebro [July–November 1938], when many of our people were killed, we almost began to accept it as inevitable. I don't think we were callous – it was just part of life. We knew something of the murders and tortures, and the killings of the Republicans when the Franco forces over-ran a village or town, and we expected that to happen if the Fascists won.

When I had the lorry it was always a feature that, wherever

you went, you would see somebody sitting on the roadside thumbing a lift. Of course we always did what we could, unless we happened to be in a hurry. The moment you stopped to pick up someone, within a matter of seconds ten or fifteen would appear with their goats, hens and chickens. This was a feature of any journey we made in an open lorry. On the ambulance, of course, it was different. Nobody ever tried to stop an ambulance, and with the motorbike it was altogether quite different because I was alone. I did have a pillion and there were occasions when I took passengers. On a long journey – I didn't have a speedometer on the motor-bike – to kill time I would either sing all the songs I knew, or try to count the telephone posts and guess how far I had gone, and work out the speed. I had a map then, but it wasn't very clear.

It was always very exciting to go to Albacete, the base of the International Brigades. Brigaders were arriving from all over the world and in the canteen you would hear every language imaginable. Again, I was always in the position where, if I wanted to go to the canteen, I would never do so unless I got my bike looked after by one of the guards or policemen. I wasn't a good mechanic but I knew how to service the bike. There was one occasion – the bike was a twin Douglas – when one of the gaskets blew and there were some flames coming from one part. I must have been twenty or thirty miles away from the nearest town and I drove along with one leg in the air so it didn't get burnt. I managed to limp into this place, and of course they didn't have a gasket head or whatever it was and we had to improvise. Improvising was a very important part of the whole transport problem. I knew little but managed to service the lorry, the ambulance and the bike, and we kept them on the road all the time I was there.

I had one accident on the bike going round a sharp bend. I came off. There was a fairly deep drop the other side and I went rolling down with the bike on top of me. I managed to clear the bike, but my arm was badly hurt. I didn't know whether it was broken or not – I didn't have any feeling in it. I must have stayed there for two or three hours before somebody came along to help me. In the event I was OK – they managed to get the bike onto a lorry and get me back to the hospital, and I think it was two or three weeks before I could use it fully, and was able to drive again.

There was one woman in the hospital named Winifred Bates, the wife of Ralph Bates, the famous author of *The Olive Field*, 1936, among others. She used to do some reporting, and occasionally I would take her to different parts of Spain, Barcelona particularly, where she had to link up with people she was working for. She wrote a pamphlet about the British Medical Unit. Things were quiet at the time, and they asked me if I would go back to England with the pamphlet to get it printed and also to take part in the campaign in Fleet Street for the sending of a further ambulance from Fleet Street.

What always struck me was that, when men came into the hospital wounded, I can't ever remember anybody feeling despair or wishing they hadn't come. There was a feeling of confidence. We never thought we would ever lose the war because there was such massive support among the people of Spain. We all did our best to keep in touch with whatever organisations we were from, and letters from Britain were very widely circulated. We also got copies of the *Daily Worker*.

The roads in Spain were full of holes and one night we took some wounded to the hospital. I remember the men lying there, very badly wounded, screaming that I was a Fascist and trying to kill them by going over the ruts in the road. On that particular occasion we didn't have any nurse or staff to accompany the wounded. I had to do what I could myself – but there was very little I *could* do. Anyway, we got them back safely and they all not only survived, but, within a matter of months, and sometimes weeks, they were back in the line.

I wrote fairly regularly to the Party branch and to individual members. I remember once writing to NATSOPA [National Society of Operative Printers and Assistants] and saying that we had certain shortages, like chocolate, soap, toilet rolls and cigarettes. Cigarettes were the thing we wanted most. One day a great big tea chest arrived for me. It was customary when anybody received a parcel that everybody gathered around because, whatever it was, we shared it. We were all agog – what could be in this big tea chest? When I opened it up, it was toilet rolls and soap – but a week or two later we got parcels of cigarettes and chocolate. The food we had through the whole of the period was inadequate, but we expected that. We lived on beans, I think more than anything else. I didn't mind – I have always liked beans. But they were usually cooked in garlic and olive oil and there were some from the British Battalion who just couldn't stomach it. There was one bloke who went for days on bread only. There were others like him who couldn't manage the food. Lots of them were very inadequately fed and you could see it in their faces at times, but it never depressed them – it didn't affect our morale. As I said, we never thought we would ever lose the war.

I remember how some of the members of the Brigade, as soon as they were fit enough to walk and get about, were always eager to go back to the unit – to the battalion. I remember the feeling of pride among the staff in the hospital when patients were able to walk and be mobile. Lilian, who worked as a masseuse and nurse, was faced with the problem of trying to help the soldiers to walk again. She designed a gadget that had three sides to it: people could lean on it and it would help them to stagger along.

I remember how we coped with the cold. They say of the plain of Madrid that the wind is not strong enough to blow out a candle, yet strong enough to kill a man. Two or three times, when we went to Madrid or Albacete in the height of the winter period, it was so cold, unbelievably cold; I had never experienced anything like it. On one occasion we were on a lorry, going down a very steep hill. The wind was icy, and a whole number of lorries and ambulances had gone into a ditch. I had a spare driver with me, he drove in bottom gear and four of us tied a rope to the back of the lorry – walked down behind it, trying to keep the back of the lorry from sliding into the ditch, and we succeeded.

I remember the trip we had around Spain, trying to deliver the parcels which had been collected in England for Christmas of 1937, and the joy of people who were in isolated parts of the battlefront to get some goodies. Wherever we went, they were delighted to see us. The whole trip left a vague memory of various places, because, whenever we stopped, we had to see the mayor of the village or the town, and their kindness was always overwhelming. They were having a hard time themselves and yet they always tried to help us and feed us – although we avoided it as much as we could, knowing how short they were themselves.

It was September 1938 when I came back to raise funds for an ambulance – back to the East End. The Brigade had contacted the printers – they had an organisation, the Printers' Anti-Fascist Movement, and raised money for an ambulance. To do that they went to all the Chapels – we even got some money from [press baron Lord] Beaverbrook. We had regular meetings with several wounded who had been returned.

We raised the money but by that time the war had changed and they wired us that they didn't want an ambulance; they wanted a lorry, with as much medical equipment as we could get. So we gathered all the money we had and made another appeal to all the Chapels and got quite a lot more. Two other printers and I were going to take it over to Benicasim, to the headquarters of Medical Aid. But we were stuck at the border for a while, and that's when we saw all these people flooding towards us. We arrived back at about the time the first refugees reached the Spanish border. They increased in numbers and, when they got to the French border, the French gendarmes made them lay down their arms, so they had great piles of arms – and they didn't give them any help, any water or any food. They were near starving – there were hundreds and thousands of refugees with no food – so the reporters Bill Forrest and Tom Driberg telephoned London and reported about the way French authorities were treating refugees – which got front-page stories in the *Daily Express* and the *News Chronicle*.

They let them into France, but there were no facilities for them at all. The first wave were people who had been in hospital so we took them to nearby hospitals. We did two or three trips. We saw the wounded and children being carried. We saw photos used in the propaganda of women carrying babies that were already dead. We never saw that ourselves, but what we did see, and we stopped to photograph her, was a woman helping the Spanish women whose babies had died. By that time they were near starvation, and they'd been three or four days on the frontier without any food. The articles by Bill Forrest and Tom Driberg created quite a sensation. They reported that refugees needed food quickly, but the French sent the gendarmes to keep them down and wouldn't allow any food to be brought in. We'd been given £50 each to live on while we were out there, and we went and bought loads of bread and chocolate – but they wouldn't take any money. We started sharing out the chocolate – and we'd bought about five hundred loaves and we cut them in half and started giving them out. There was nearly a riot.

After the civil war there were all these Basque children who had been evacuated to the UK. I'd taken thirty to Hammersmith and the Committee arranged to put the children up in homes of the volunteers. After Barcelona and Madrid fell, the Fascists were cock-a-hoop – Franco got in touch with the United Nations demanding that the Basque children be returned. The Party said they'd send the first lot back and I was to take them. I took thirty of them back to the border, across the river. I was in charge with some Red Cross officials. I sent messages across the river to them about the children. They wanted to know when we'd be sending the children across. I took the decision that we weren't going to unless we had a letter from each of their parents. All the children were talking and there was terrible sadness among them. These were the children who'd left when they were ten and eleven year olds and now were thirteen and fourteen and had come from peaceful England to a Fascist state. We absolutely refused to send them back unless we got a letter from their parents. They arrived back late in the day with the letters. Sometimes I cry when I think of it, the children hanging onto me, not wanting to go. It took all day. They all went back and we never saw any of them again.

When the last members of the battalion arrived at Victoria, there was such joy, the celebration, the tremendous enthusiasm of the crowd. Later on we went to a meeting somewhere in central London. It was after that that the depression set in for me, the realisation that we had lost the war – that Fascism had been victorious – and I thought of all the losses, the thousands of Brigaders and, of course, I thought of Spanish Republicans and what they were going through, the imprisonment, the torture and the killings.

After all these sacrifices, did we achieve anything? I think we did! I am proud of having gone and I would do it all again.

PENNY FEIWEL

Born 24 April 1909 in Tottenham, north London

My father was known in the neighbourhood as 'Punch' Phelps. He was an unskilled labourer, like most of the men in our street – a jack-of-all-trades, master of none. He was in and out of jobs, as a navvy on the roads, on buildings or in the railway yards. He was a chirpy, kindly man, always optimistic and full of backchat, never harbouring a grudge – but he had to work terribly hard, and in some jobs, I remember, he was driven so hard that after leaving the house at four in the morning he would come back in the afternoon drenched in sweat and dead tired, throw himself on his bed and fall asleep.

He was a rough diamond, but he wasn't spiteful. He had a hard life, and he worked very, very hard, too – but he was always good to us children. He used to get up early in the morning before he went to his job as a navvy, and he'd clean

all our shoes before we went to school. He never hit us –
he used to say, 'I'll aim half a crown at you.' We'd laugh at
that – but his attitude would be threatening. My mother was
very short-tempered. I had many a black eye from her – but
she had a hard life. She was one girl among thirteen brothers,
so she had to learn to look after herself. Her family were
shopkeepers – they used to deliver coal on carts and they
had a greengrocery shop as well. Right until I grew up,
they kept that shop – amazing. My mother had stamina – but,
my goodness, she had a temper. In my mind's eye I carry
a picture of her with jet-black hair covered by a man's cloth
cap, a white blouse and a long black ragged skirt, a piece of
coarse sacking tied round her waist in place of an apron, and
wearing boots done up with side buttons and with a broom
in her hand.

There were a lot of us, but my mother adopted a boy; her
friend who had a child died in the workhouse, and my
mother took the baby and brought him up. He lived with us,
but my eldest sister, Violet didn't get on with him. In Edith
Road – and it was usually the same in the other places we
lived (because several times we had to leave after falling into
arrears with the rent) – we had three rooms: a kitchen/living
room with the grate and sink where the lot of us had our
meals, washed and sat about, and two bedrooms. A gas meter
was laid on, but such a thing as a bathroom was unheard of.
Most of our neighbours lived in the same way.

I have a picture of women, wearing their husbands' caps,
talking across the road from their front doors, some of them

48

leaning on their brooms, others scrubbing their front steps with buckets of water. The houses just could not be kept clean, because the children were always rushing in and out, and there were no street cleaners in those days – at least not in our area. The dust and dirt from the streets outside and smoke from the railway and the factories blew in so much that in summer our windows were often kept tightly closed. In winter there was the damp, against which one could do nothing. Whenever possible, us kids were sent into the street so that we swarmed around the pavements.

To us the pawnshop was important – on the Saturday our best clothes were taken out to wear on Sunday, then they were back in again on Monday. My mother even used to pawn her wedding ring and her Sunday clothes; thankfully those days have gone now, but we were always in the pawnshop. I hated it. To make a few pennies we sold bunches of mint in West Green Road by the kerb, at a penny a bunch. We had a garden and my father used to grow mint and carrots. When the carrots got so high, my brother and I would dig them up, take the tops off and wash them in the butt outside, and stick the stalks back again in the soil – and take the carrots to school. One day I got caught going underneath my desk to eat a piece of carrot. The teacher caught me and said, 'Bring out what you're eating.' I emptied all these carrots onto the floor. She said, 'I never knew we had a donkey in the class.'

Dad went into the army in 1914. I remember my mother hanging out the washing in the garden at the time, when my pa came to go, and I don't know what he said, but I saw her wiping her eyes with her apron. From then on my mother had to carry the whole burden, so, soon after he was gone, she went to work in a munitions factory. In a brown overall and with a mob cap covering her jet-black hair, she'd go off early in the morning, coming home dead tired in the evening. It was a trying time for her because, before setting off for work, she had to get the five of us ready for school before the first factory whistle. Bill, the eldest, was in the top form, while I, at five or so, was sent along with the others, and a neighbour looked after Rosie, the baby. War at first seemed quite exciting to us children in Tottenham, with talk of heroes and our British navy, and the enemy Hun, but soon there were food cards and, before going to school, we had to queue up outside food shops, which I hated. There were free meals at school – usually pea soup or stew dumpling – but it wasn't sufficient, and by evening we were hungry. Often my mother hadn't enough food for us, and I can remember many nights when my brother and I stood outside the factories, especially the Harris Lebus furniture factory in Ferry Lane, waiting for the people to come out from various shifts, holding out our hands for any bits of their lunch they had left over. Often we were in luck, getting half a sandwich or a piece of bread and cheese.

I had to go into hospital, because I had a fall. It was a severe winter – one of the worst winters we'd ever known – and my mother was working in Leavis's factory. For this she needed hairpins, as she had long hair. It was early in the morning, she was going to work and the factory hooter was going – and she hadn't any hairpins – so she got my young brother and said, 'You go and get me some hairpins. And mind how you go – it's very slippery.'

He got as far as the iron gate and he fell and came back. So she got me and said, '*You* go now and see if you can keep your feet properly.' So I went. I didn't slip, but I knocked my elbow very badly. But I carried on, got her hairpins and came back, but the elbow was very bad. My mother went off to work, but when I was at school there was the teacher doing the PE exercises, and she pulled my arm up and I winced. She said, 'What are you wincing for? What's the matter with you?'

And I said, 'I banged it on my way out.'

She looked at it and said, 'I'd better write a letter to your mother to take you to the doctor.'

My mother took me to the Tottenham hospital, and they kept me in and operated on me. They discovered a diseased bone, which was operated on twice, and I was in hospital for quite a long time with osteomyelitis. I've still got the scars.

When I came out, my father, who had been ill with pneumonia, was invalided home from France and sent to a Redhill convalescent home. He was a very good cook in the army and they allowed me to go and help him during the daytime. He had a landlady who looked after him and me of a night and I had a wonderful time there in Redhill. We used to go blackberrying with his chums and the landlady. When I came home, the nurse used to come and dress my wound. My father stayed there, cooking for the Redhill barracks, until he was invalided out of the army, and my time there was an interval of freedom I never forgot.

It was during a Zeppelin air raid that my brother Georgie was born. There were now two babies instead of one. For some reason, my older brother and sister were always scrapping with each other, and, besides, Jim was a boy, so that I had most of the responsibility for looking after my young sister, Rosie, and Georgie, the baby. Oh Lord, what a burden it was! What I remember now of the war years is not the excitement, and not even standing in the food queues, but always being saddled with these two unfortunate kids wherever I went. Soon after Georgie was born, I began missing days at school. I now slept with two others in one small bed and got so little sleep that I often dropped off during class. In this way I was soon the dunce at school and, because I lost my temper when the teachers spoke sharply to me, I became sullen and obstinate – even though I didn't want to be.

On 14 July 1919 an election was held in our district, and voting cars with huge posters were touring the streets, telling people like my parents – who knew nothing of politics or social conditions – who they were to vote for. We children were playing out in the streets and somebody dared me to jump on the back of one of the voting cars, which was moving pretty fast. Because I was always game for a dare, I did, and hung on and turned my head back triumphantly. But, just as I did so, I looked straight at an enormous police-man standing on the kerb not six feet away, who gave me such a glare that in my terror I let go, falling flat on the paving stones and grazing my arms and knees so badly that once again I was taken off to hospital to have my cuts and grazes dressed. This took time, and when I came home late, creeping quietly through the door for fear of the hiding I thought was in store for me, I had a new surprise. My mother's room was locked again, the house was full of neighbours and I was told I had just been presented with twin brothers! My mother had been told I'd been run over, and the shock had precipitated the birth. I don't know why I hadn't realised she was pregnant – somehow lots of children never did. But when I heard the news – not only one new baby but two – everything seemed to go black before my eyes, and in my mind, too. Now I would never be free. It would always be like this. I just went out and sat on the doorstep, though my cuts and bruises were still sore, and I wept and wept. Now, instead of having two youngsters to look after, I had four.

Nearly all my memories are connected with the pram my mother bought on the never-never [a system of hire purchase], pushing the old thing up and down the street with two kids inside and a third one hanging onto the crossbar below, and a fourth one perhaps hanging onto my frock; if ever I tried to park them and sneak off on my own, there would be loud yells and I would have to dash back to them.

I had got interested in my schoolwork, but now it was goodbye to any hopes I had of catching up with my lessons so that school hours shouldn't be such a misery to me. With so many kids at home, I felt I hadn't a chance, and the least thing made me feel bitter and resentful. Everything was against me.

At school I could never make up for the days I had missed. When figures were on the blackboard I didn't know whether to go upwards or downwards, or start at the pounds end or the farthings. I was usually tired and my mind used to go quite blank, as though I wasn't seeing anything on the blackboard, and when asked a question I just became sullen. Certain teachers disliked me because I seemed dull and backward.

One teacher was always making me a laughing stock. She used to stand me up before all the class and ask me questions I couldn't answer, so I just remained dumb, or said I had forgotten – which angered her so that she often caned me. One day, when I didn't answer she said, 'Come up here, Phelps,' as she advanced towards me with her cane.

At that, rage seized me, and I picked up an inkpot. The whole room gasped, including the teacher.

Then she said, 'How dare you, Phelps? Put that down.'

I said, 'I'll dare anything if you touch me with that stick again.'

She still advanced towards me with the cane, so I shied the ink bottle straight at her. The bottle didn't hit her, but all the ink did. My goodness: what a mess, all over her dress and the room. I got caned for this – but by the headmistress herself – and I was given a letter to take home to my father.

When the twins were born I was much older; we were a large family, always quarrelling – but we always made up afterwards. We used to play rounders, skipping, and the boys used to join in the skipping. And we played hide-and-seek and touch. I was always a daredevil – with all my brothers I was up to scratch with them. All the same, I used to be scared stiff of my own shadow. In those days they used to keep the dead at home in their coffin and put them on the table in the parlour – and shut the door. My brothers knew I was scared of shadows and the dark, and I would never go into the parlour on my own. I had a feeling that there was something in that end room and that I mustn't go in. I think it was a thing between me and my sister, little Emily, who died. I knew there was something in that room that I didn't understand – and I used to toddle to the door and get just up to the handle, then I'd be pulled away sharply. That was a shock to me. I didn't know what I was doing – just turning the handle – but as I opened the door it was very dark, then someone pulled me aside. From that time on I was afraid of the dark, until I was quite old – even until going up to nursing. It was only night nursing that cured me.

I left school at thirteen. When you left school you were supposed to produce your birth certificate, and the teacher said to me, 'I haven't got your birth certificate – I must have it.'

So I said to my mother, 'I want my birth certificate.'

She said, 'I'll have to go and get it.' Everything was always, 'I'll get it.'

Days and weeks went by and still she was 'going to get it'. She never got it – so at the end of term I just left and never went back.

When I was a kid of just thirteen, my mother made me

put my hair up and sent me into service. It was in Orpington, and to me it was like being on the other side of the world. I was scared of my own shadow even then. I used to write to her, 'Please take me out of here.' I would get up in the early hours of the morning to whitewash the steps and blacklead the kitchen ovens. It was cheap slave labour. But eventually my mother did come and bring me home – and then I started going into factories.

The Eagle Pencil factory was one of the first ones, but my mother took me away from there. Getting work for children was easy – it was the grown-ups who found it difficult. So I would join another factory making pencils or furniture. I went on to Leavis's furniture, where I used to push heavy furniture – plane it – then go over it, fill up the cracks, and then push it on further, through all the stages of polishing. It was very hard work but I quite enjoyed it because I was making contact with other girls. Always being new at a job was hateful. I couldn't settle down, and in between there was so much housework and looking after the children that I was glad to be off again. But all the jobs were blind alleys leading me nowhere, and when I discovered I had left school a year too soon I felt really bitter towards my parents.

I loved crochet and needlework. I used to make loads of lace and tray cloths for neighbours – they'd buy the cotton and I'd make it for a few pence. Even up until recently I was still doing cloths for people. I've still got some of the little bits of lace and tray cloths. I did wide lace for the church, too. I used to go to the park opposite the Prince of Wales Hospital,

Tottenham, and I'd sit there with the twins and crochet, while my mother was doing her washing. I used to see the nurses come out and walk round to their home.

There was a lady in the road who used to do dressmaking, and take her stuff to the West End in London. She would employ a few girls like me and my neighbour to sew at her house. It was slave labour, really – a sweatshop. She was a very good dressmaker and she did all the D'Oyly Carte Company's dresses – beautiful costumes – and she taught me how to do fly-running stitch. After I went into the hospital at Charing Cross as a student, I used to get theatre tickets from Theatreland, and I'd see the D'Oyly Carte and wonder if those costumes were stitched by me.

Of a Sunday, all us crowd were at home. My mother and father used to like to have a sleep after dinner – and we used to be sent off. I was a bit of a rebel – no angel – and I could fight as well as my brothers. It was nothing for me to be in a fight with one of my brothers and him getting the worst of it. Not far from us, in Broad Lane, stood the corrugated tin chapel of the Plymouth Brethren – I suppose the strictest Christian sect in England – bearing a board on which was written, 'How shall I be saved? Believe in the Lord Jesus Christ and thou SHALT be saved'.

I had always been sent to Sunday School, chiefly because my mother didn't know what to do with us on Sunday afternoons after the midday meal. At Sunday School we sang hymns and learnt Bible lessons, and finally I became converted to the Plymouth Brethren. For three years I kept every rule and belief of what I was told was the only Christian religion that could help me be saved. I never went to the pictures, nor to dances, never went walking with boys, stopped swearing and even thought I ought to change my job because it was sinful to be working on stage clothes. In a way, this religion and denying myself all worldly pleasures, as even cinemas were called, was a passive rebellion against my environment, and gave me a sense of virtue and satisfaction. At home I acted superior, and was sneered at and laughed at, and was nicknamed 'the Bible-Puncher'. Looking back, I think I must have been an awful prig, but I still have a soft spot for the Plymouth Brethren. In a poor and ignorant district like ours they did a tremendous amount of good.

Through religion I taught myself self-control, which was all to the good. I came to mix with people who spoke better English than I did, and I learnt to imitate them. I was also encouraged to better my education and go to evening classes. On the other hand, I was among a lot of pretty badly repressed women, with no outlet for their emotions, leading monotonous lives, and apt to turn queer and bitter, making me in some ways even more repressed and unnatural than I was before.

One of the teachers befriended me and took me under her wing. She used to invite me to her house after Sunday School for tea, and in the evening she would take me home. There was another one who was very motherly, and who had a daughter, and I used to try to imitate her. She went to the Tottenham High School and, me being a cockney, I used anything but the right words, so she always used to correct me. I always remember learning my first words of French with her, which were *'Fermez la porte, s'il vous plaît'* – she was just a young kid, but she taught me.

That stayed with me – and so did the Scriptures. I can still quote the Bible – but I never felt right into it, although I used to go to Bible-preaching meetings, and it did have an influence on me. I got very attached to the people, so even when I went into nursing I stayed in touch with them. I have a lot to thank those outside influences for. Somehow I always came under the influence of the right type of people. There was one Sunday School teacher who worked in a good position in a factory, and I asked her if I could join – but she said no, I shouldn't go into factory work.

As I got older I got fed up with the job I was doing – it was no good. I didn't make friends very easily. There were two other girls – and there was always an odd one out, and that was me. I used to pass these roads to the factory and see the girls working in the offices, and I used to think, 'I'd like to do that – do some typing'. I went round to the school and they said I could join for shorthand and typing – and I was very keen and worked really hard. I was determined to make up for the schooling I had not made use of or missed altogether, and at the chapel I was encouraged to do this. I was fifteen when I first went to evening classes. I was one of the keenest attendees. We had no exams, but weekly tests, and to my surprise I found I often came out top.

There was a Mr Turner, and, at the end of the period, he

would give away free theatre tickets to the one who came top. I always seemed to be getting the theatre tickets – but I never went to the theatre because I was a Plymouth Brethren and you didn't go to theatres and you didn't go with boys – so I used to give them away.

One day Mr Turner said, while he was marking our notes: 'Tell me, Miss Phelps, I'm very curious – you don't use your theatre tickets, do you?'

I thought I'd been caught out, but I said, 'No sir.'

He asked 'Why not?'

I said, 'Because I'm a Plymouth Brethren, and we don't go to the theatre.'

'Oh, I see.'

So he left it at that for the time being, but another time he said, 'Miss Phelps, would you like to come home to lunch with us? I'll give you an address to meet you on a Sunday.' It was some station in central London.

So I went home, and my elder sister was very suspicious of young girls and young men, and she said to my mother, 'You're not going to let her go at her age – to meet a man at a station, who'll pretend he's going to take her home for lunch?'

I said, 'But he is.'

But she said, 'Don't you believe her.' And my mother took her side and wouldn't let me go.

I didn't quite know what to do. I couldn't go back to school in the evening for quite a while, but eventually I plucked up courage. I knew I was going to tell a lie – and I met Mr

Turner, and he said, 'Miss Phelps, I'm sorry we missed you.'

And I said, 'I didn't know your address or where you lived, so I couldn't tell you that I wasn't well.' That was the only excuse I could make.

He said, 'Oh, well, perhaps another time,' but, from that time on, when he mentioned the wife, that made me mad – because I had a very quick temper.

When I got home I went for my sister. I said, 'He wasn't trying it on – he was married and had a nice wife – and they went there to meet me, and you spoilt it all.' But still he took an interest in me, and so did his wife – they were the first people who really encouraged me.

During the next two years I visited the Turners frequently, and both Mr and Mrs Turner continued to take a real interest in my career, helping with all possible advice. Mrs Turner helped me to become more human by getting me to moderate my religious tendencies. I had always said cinemas were sinful, but Mrs Turner said she could see I was not happy – that I oughtn't to go on leading a dull and uninteresting life. I denied this, saying that I was perfectly happy – but without conviction. Then, one day, I broke the rule and went with the Turners to the cinema, feeling frightfully guilty about it, but very soon this sense of guilt passed. Once I had broken through this one restriction, others went too, though it was still some years before I went to the theatre.

One day Mr Turner said to me 'Miss Phelps, wouldn't you like to change your job from working in factories?'

I said, 'What can I do?'

He said, 'You could do an office job.'

I said, 'But I'm not trained to do it – the arithmetic.' But he and his wife helped me quite a lot.

Then, one evening, with the Turners' advice, I made the decision to try to become a nurse. I was of an age now to do nursing, and I applied to the Homerton Hospital to do that because they took people a bit younger. I was too young for general nursing training, but not too young to do fever nursing. Following my application, I received a letter telling me I had been accepted on trial as a probationer nurse. This was January 1928. Living inside a big hospital, being part of its life and wearing its uniform, opened quite a new world for me. Now I had at last done what I wanted, and I seemed at once cut off from the life of our home and our street. At home the family doubted my chances, and said I was suffering with a swollen head if I thought I could go through with it – and I thought so myself – but I worked hard at the hospital and kept very quiet. The work was tiring, but I found it interesting and made good progress, particularly on the practical side. In the qualifying examinations at the end of the year I managed to come out top.

I got on very well. I only missed getting a medal by four marks for being half an hour late – and I'll tell you what made me late. We didn't have buses or taxis in those days – it was trams from Hackney down to Seven Sisters Road and down to Amhurst Road. I was playing tennis that morning in the grounds of the hospital at Homerton, and the sister passed by and I was representing the nurses, being the one picked out to compete with other nurses at the hospital. She saw me and said, 'Nurse Phelps, don't you be late!'

And I said, 'I won't, Sister.'

I was enjoying my game of tennis – but when I went I didn't realise that buses didn't run and it was just trams, and I was a bit late and I started to run. I never ran so much in my whole life as I did then but I arrived half an hour late – and when I went in I was sweating because I'd run all the way. The matron used to say I was a good runner, and I got to the hospital and found the room. The sister was sitting there, supervising the nurses, and she pointed to the first chair, so I went in – boiling – and sat down. She never even came and gave me a drink of water. I started reading, and the first words I caught were 'oculogyral spasms', which I knew about, and I was writing and I went all through that paper, and I was bang on time. It was over and the bell went to stop, and, instead of going to the top, she came to me first to collect my paper. I was just on the last sentence, and she wouldn't let me finish – she was really a nasty bit of work – because I could have completed that last one. I knew about oculogyral spasms. But she took it away and so I lost out on the medal by four marks, for being half an hour late. I got higher marks than the medallist in the practical and oral – but I still didn't get the medal.

For nearly five years I worked as staff nurse at different hospitals, but I was never altogether content because, after a while, hospital routine didn't satisfy me. It was the social conditions attached to nursing that got me down. In my early years, a nurse's pay was ridiculously small and the hours terribly long, and worst of all was the snobbish and hypocritical discipline, which I thought an insult to any intelligent woman. It was just exploitation. Nurses were often spoken to by members of the senior staff in a tone no factory girl would have put up with. What irritated me most of all was that, on duty, a nurse was supposed to be a woman with enough brains to carry responsibility, but off duty we were treated like children. We were given hardly any free time and made to keep absurd rules, particularly about seeing men friends, and all because of the Victorian tradition that nursing wasn't work – it was a noble sacrifice – so we could dispense with decent hours and pay.

I finished my hospital training – I came top in the hospital – then I went on to apply to voluntary hospitals. I applied to one of the best hospitals in London but I hadn't had the secondary education for it. It didn't matter what my hospital experience was, even though I nearly always came out top. Eventually I applied to Charing Cross, and they *did* take me. I asked to have a talk with the matron before the interview. She was a motherly sort, and I was candid with her. She said she could quite understand how I felt – and she said she would give me a chance. 'You can go to the hospital training school and see how you go – but if you're no good, you'll have to leave.' And that was it. I went to Charing Cross for my training, which was a wonderful experience, and that was the beginning.

I was getting on well, but then I became very, very ill and

my mother was called. I'd been to see a friend in Brentwood and was coming home late – you had to get in by twelve o'clock at the nurses' home from your day off. I realised it was late and I was going to miss my bus to take me to Hackney, and I ran when I saw the bus coming. It slowed down and then went on again, and I ran after it, and, as I ran, I missed it and slipped. I had a big gash on my leg. Nobody had seen me fall, and I knew it was my own fault. Then a motorist came along and said he'd take me to the hospital, but I said 'no' – with my nurse's discipline, I was afraid not to get back in time – so he said he'd take me to the house where I could get something to clean my leg and put some iodine and a bandage on it. He took me as far as Hackney and I met one of my night nurses and I explained to her. She said, 'Come on, Phelps,' – they always called you by your surname – 'that needs proper dressing and stitches.' The night sister came along, bound my leg, ticked me off and put me in the sickbay.

I didn't think much of the injury, but after a while my temperature went up, and I thought my neck and face felt queer. When the doctor came, I told him I felt a queer stiffness at the back of my neck. He asked me if I was sickening for mumps, but when I told him I'd had mumps he left it at that. But that night the stiff pain got worse – at times I felt as if the muscles of my face were being pulled out of their sockets – and I couldn't breathe. Early in the morning I had some kind of convulsion. Another nurse who had served during the war was also in the sick ward. Immediately she saw my condition she ran to the telephone, calling the night nurse, 'My God, the girl's got tetanus! I saw it during the war and you can never forget it!'

The night nurse came just as I had a second convulsion. The doctor came rushing in and there was a lot of telephoning for serum. Suddenly they were charging around like mad, sending to the lab to get tetanus antitoxin. They even sent an ambulance to collect it. There was talk of desensitising me, and I was given chloroform and morphine to ease the convulsions, but all the time I was conscious and in worse pain than I had ever imagined possible. While I was given a spinal serum injection, I had such a convulsion that my hands and feet felt as if they were being torn off.

I suppose this should have been the end of me, because the survival rate for tetanus, if not treated in time, is pretty small. For a week I was critically ill, but I don't remember much about it. My mother was called and the matron said, 'You don't know what tetanus is, do you? Well, it's lockjaw', and the next thing [my mother] knew she was being given some brandy. I was very ill, but they got to me in time. Tetanus was very rampant in those days.

I returned from convalescing and told the matron that hospital routine had become empty for me. She was sympathetic and suggested I take a whole year's rest from nursing. She also knew of my home circumstances and that we had no money, and thought I shouldn't return home but look for other work. I didn't know how to set about it, but when staying with my elder sister Violet, long since married, I was lucky enough to meet Mr Turner again. He thought I should try to study and suggested I apply for a bursary at Hillcroft College for Women in Surbiton.

I found the principal there sympathetic and understanding and I told her how I felt something was lacking in my present life, and how I knew nothing about social conditions, and above all how I had great difficulties in expressing myself – which I wished to get over. She listened very patiently. I hadn't much hope, but not long afterwards I had a letter saying that, while no regular bursary was available, an unforeseen vacancy meant they could offer me a place, and with a second bursary from the Middlesex County Council I would be provided for.

They were well equipped for adult education, university and degrees. One tutor was Miss Street – who was very strong – she'd put the fear of God into you if you so much as looked at her. Then there was Miss Ashby, the Principal of Hillcroft College, a loveable, kindly, intellectual person, very gentle. Then Elsie Smith, who was a philosopher. They also took an interest and encouraged me, and they helped and influenced me a lot.

Miss Ashby took a special interest in me. She always called me 'Penelope', which wasn't my name – it was Ada Louise – but it stuck. Elsie Smith also took an interest in me. Hillcroft was a traumatic experience, a place apart where I never knew what was going on in the outside world. In a way I just didn't know how I was going to adapt myself, but I became great pals with Miss Ashby and her brother, Sir Arthur Ashby.

He used to supply me with reading matter that I would never have got elsewhere.

That was 1934. I studied at Hillcroft College for one year, taking courses in English, economics, psychology and history. It was hard work for me but, in between spells of feeling very disheartened, I learnt a lot. At last I was also growing up, shaking off my exaggerated religious views and realising how much I had missed. I made a lot of new friends there, and two of my best friends were Jewish girls. This was one of the things that opened my eyes. As kids in Tottenham we jeered and laughed at Jews, even though we hardly saw any. People were always grumbling about the Jews – they had all the money, they were awful people. I couldn't imagine having a Jew as a friend. Now I saw how wicked these prejudices were. I was beginning to think for myself, and this made me unsure, because there was so much to know. So much wrong with the world and so much confusion – I didn't know where to start. At holiday time, I never knew where to go – if I went home it was to a house full of boys so I wasn't sure what to do at the end of term-time. Miss Ashby said, 'I have a friend I was at university with – Heron. I'm very fond of her and her husband and children. You'd love it if you went and helped her a bit, because she's rather over-whelmed in her work, as well as her housework.' So I went and helped her with the children. I got very attached to Hannah, Patrick [the future painter Patrick Heron], and there was another one who was a Jesuit, very monastic. Then there was Giles, who ran a wonderful farm. I was accepted into the family and they had a great influence on me. Mr Heron had these beautiful shops in London – dressmaking shops – and the family and I became great friends. I even went to Italy with them many years later. They educated me, really. Patrick Heron – I knew all his paintings. Meeting them was a wonderful experience.

Late in 1936, after I left the Herons, I found temporary work in Hertfordshire as a nurse – but I had no security or commitment there. I was friendly with a night nurse and one evening she asked me, 'Phelps, are you off duty tomorrow?'

'Yes. Why?'

'Would you like to come and help us with the hunger marchers?'

'Who are the hunger marchers?'

'Don't you know? You're a bit green, aren't you? The hunger marchers from Wales.' I think her father was a Labour MP or in politics anyway – and she was very 'red'.

I asked her what she wanted me to do, and she said, 'Just some of your skills looking after their feet, and helping to collect food to feed them because they're walking all the way from Wales.'

I said, 'OK, I'll come when I get off duty tonight.'

So I started trying to beg, borrow or steal for the hunger marchers – and it worked very well. Three of us ran round this little town and we got the men a hall, and the local Co-op helped us, particularly with food – and so did a number of local shopkeepers. They were surprisingly sympathetic and generous. We obtained free medical supplies; the Women's

Guild, a local doctor and clergyman all agreed to help in any way they could.

The marchers, when they turned up, were the Yorkshire and Nottinghamshire contingents – about two hundred strong. I never saw such feet in all my life. Shocking. One man's feet were raw, so I took him through the back door to the most fashionable chiropodist in the town, who at once agreed to treat him for nothing. Another man – you just couldn't imagine it, his feet were so bad. I knew it was a hospital job, so I rang our ambulance and got the man taken to the hospital. I got hauled over the coals! Who called the ambulance? The porters who drove the ambulance knew me. I had to tell them my name, for them to take this man to casualty, where he was admitted. The matron called me in the morning. She said, 'Nurse Phelps, we don't employ nurses who are "red".'

I said, 'I'm not "red", Matron. I have no politics. I just thought it was the humanitarian thing to do. He needed help and he was a sick man.'

She said, 'You can't do that here – not in this hospital. There are people here, nurses, whose parents wouldn't approve of what you were doing – because I assume you are very communistic.'

I said, 'Not at all, I don't belong to any communist party. But if that's the way you feel, Matron, if you think I'm going to infiltrate the nurses, I've got no contract with you, so I'll go. Thank you, Matron.' And I walked out.

I think she was a bit flabbergasted. I told one of the

girls about it and she said, 'Good. If you leave, would you volunteer for Spain?'

I said I knew nothing about Spain – I didn't know anything.

She said I wanted educating, so she told me all about Spain – how the nuns were taking Franco's side, and, of course, it grabbed my heart – I was young and very emotional. She told me, 'You go to London, go to Tottenham Court Road, and you'll see the people – the Spanish Medical Aid. Talk to them.'

So that was that, and that was when I first met my boss, I always remember him – Goryan. I think he must have been Yugoslav or similar – I never knew, but you never worried what nationality or political party people belonged to. Goryan was very good. He asked me all about my nursing – did I know anything about theatre work? We used to get amputations in 'surgical' from accidents, being in central London – so we had lots of accidents. I'd had wonderful theatre experience at Charing Cross, so I said, 'Yes, I know a lot about theatre work, I worked at . . .' But that was enough.

'Well, you're going somewhere where you'll be very, very busy.'

Despite my theatre experience, the Spanish Medical Aid people still wanted me to do a radiology training course. 'No, surgery is my calling, that's what I'm good at because I worked in theatre.' That seemed to suit them, so they handed me my ticket, and I was off.

On 6 January 1937 I left England as one of a party of four English nurses to report for duty with the Spanish Medical Aid Committee in Barcelona. Setting out was exciting enough for me because I had never been abroad before – not even set foot on board ship.

We went to France, were put up overnight and mooched around the next day – we wasted practically two days in France – but we had to get paperwork filled in. Then we boarded a train for Spain. It was a terrible, terrible journey into Spain to Port-Bou – which was a horrible place.

We arrived at the frontier at one o'clock, and we had our first experience of the war. The carriage next to ours in the train that was to take us to Barcelona was badly smashed and battered, and, while we waited, we saw our first aerial bombardment. It was far out to sea – the ships and planes were almost out of sight, the sound of the guns was faint – but the Spaniards were very excited, running about and pointing, with shouts of *'Aviones! Aviones!'* – all for very little, it seemed to me. While waiting, we sat in the sun outside a little open-air restaurant, where we had a meal of meat, rice, olives, fruit and coffee.

When the train at last arrived it had funny open carriages with wooden benches, and we didn't have much room for ourselves and our luggage. It was mostly full of soldiers, and at each station on the line the train stopped and more Spanish soldiers got in, with much shouting and waving of handkerchiefs, while peasants and girls along the platform handed out armfuls of oranges to anyone who wanted them.

We were altogether three days in Barcelona. In the shops, food didn't seem very plentiful, but I thought clothes were cheap, and our taxi was certainly the cheapest we had ever been in. There were hardly any signs of war, but still, as compared to other towns I had known, there was an air of tension about.

We made our way to the station with all our luggage – probably no one had ever gone to Spain as well equipped as we were. We had sleeping bags, leather leggings, boiler suits, blankets, nurses' overalls, gas masks and various utensils. But, oh dear, when we got to the station! Inexperienced as we were, we didn't yet know that this was wartime, and that people might already have been waiting the whole day to make sure of getting a place. The train was crammed full, with soldiers occupying every inch of the corridors, and one glance showed there wasn't an earthly hope of getting all our luggage in. Our temporary organiser, who didn't strike me as likely to organise anything, was in despair. He said it would be absurd to think we needed so much luggage, and he made us leave behind – of all things – our leggings, boiler suits, sleeping bags and blankets . . . in fact all the things we would later miss bitterly. He promised to send them after us, but of course we never saw any of it again.

In Valencia we had to change trains, and the train to Albacete was even fuller than the coastal train. As we drew away from the coast, it got colder. We stopped at all kinds of little stations, where crowds of villagers brought offerings of fruit for the soldiers – mostly oranges. I've never seen so much fruit in my life.

We pushed on to Albacete, where, after a long, cold wait, a guard came and took us halfway across the town to a place where an official in a badly lit office said a few words in English to us. From there we were taken to a hospital and put into an empty and freezing-cold ward, where we tried to wrap ourselves into blankets and get a little sleep. The smell of the latrines was terrific, everything was filthy and dirty and we were next door to the lavatories. I never slept that night. There was not just one in a bed – there were two or three – and sometimes you found yourself moving around; well, it was so full of people, and you'd say 'move over – make room, I'm tired', and you'd find yourself sleeping among a whole load of men. It was amazing to me. Gosh, what a terrible place that was! I think everyone knew Albacete. Shocking. We seemed to be stuck there – we couldn't move until our papers arrived and it wasn't just a couple of hours; you could hang around for days. You used to get vouchers for this and vouchers for that.

Albacete was the base of the International Brigades and was a bewildering military camp. We went from one supposed authority in charge to another. No one seemed to know anything about us – where we were supposed to go or stay. The main language in the International Brigades at this time was German, and then French. Scarcely anyone spoke a word of English, and I could sense at once that the English were not particularly liked.

At last an American doctor telephoned and found a room for us in the Hotel Nacional – a small hotel in a back street – and the front streets weren't up to much. Our room was small, dark and filthy, with three narrow beds, placed right next to the lavatory, which had ceased to work, and the smell from which was overpowering. We tried to get away from this smell as much as we could, but smells of one kind or another could not be avoided in overcrowded Albacete.

On the third day, at last, we saw two Austrians who were in charge – Dr Neumann and Dr Talger – who spoke fair English. Here we were told we would be separated. Mrs Murphy would go to the Madrid Front and the other girl and I were told to report for duty at the international base hospital just started in Murcia. We were told that some wounded men would be evacuated to Murcia in the afternoon train, and we would be in charge of their evacuation.

When we got to the station we had a shock. Instead of the few wounded I had imagined, there were well over a hundred men: a few quite badly wounded, and some lighter cases – arms, legs and flesh wounds.

It was a terrible journey. It got dark and cold, and the train was so slow I sometimes wanted to get out and push. I tried to give attention to those who needed it, but most of the men were drinking wine and singing, and thought an *enfermera* [a nurse] – especially an English *enfermera* – a great joke.

At Murcia I was put in charge of my own general ward, but instead of an ordinary ward I found myself in a huge lecture hall, with endless rows of tightly placed beds. There must have been a good two hundred beds, all occupied and mostly by French patients. Some were badly wounded; others had little the matter with them except mysterious aches and pains. A few of them, I think, were just swinging the lead.

For the first two days, and practically all night, I was on the run, frantically trying to establish order, taking temperatures, bringing water and changing bandages. Those who could walk used to disappear and come back after a while with bottles of wine, and begin to sing, until I lost my temper and hushed them. In the meantime I tried to attend to those patients who really needed care. There was one man who had both arms off – he had to be fed, but he was one of the gentlest and bravest patients I had in Spain.

I had been in Murcia nearly a week when I saw a dark man, who stood for some time at the end of the ward, watching me work. Later a messenger from Albacete arrived and asked how I was getting on. I said I felt rather wasted, because I had good surgical experience, and I had done nothing except introduce a bit of order and discipline – which anybody could have done. He told me that Goryan, the medical chief, was looking for a theatre nurse, and I should go to the Grand Hotel that evening for an interview.

I was shown into a room at the hotel where a middle-aged man with a very high forehead, long, dark hair and a big, dark moustache, wearing a sheepskin coat, was sitting at a table talking to some officers in uniform. This was Goryan, and I recognised him as the man who had watched me in the ward earlier that day – and who had interviewed me in London. He questioned me again about my experience, and at the end he said I would be attached to the 11th Brigade, composed mainly of the Thaelmann Battalion, and I was to get my permit to travel with him at seven sharp the next morning.

Our headquarters were in a big barn, right next to the well, in the shadow of the tall cliff. We had no running water, and large pitchers were passed round from mouth to mouth. All night dispatch riders came with messages for Goryan – then a decisive message came. Goryan looked set, and gave quick orders in French and Spanish. The battle was on. As we moved off towards our station on the front I heard the sound of guns getting louder with the growing light of day.

We travelled till it was bright daylight, but making only slow progress, because every few miles we seemed to have to stop and take shelter to escape the attention of enemy planes. During one of these halts in a small village, my long hair was cut off short, like a boy's, at the suggestion of one of the doctors, who thought it would get in the way.

Wounded had already been evacuated to Tarancón, and its two hospitals were full. We took charge of an empty school and at once set to, preparing a theatre, unloading our equipment and scrubbing and disinfecting floors and walls.

We had no running water in the building, but we fixed up big chromium containers for boiling water and we fixed up our electricity. Before we were half-ready, the first ambulance drew up outside, unloading its wounded. At the door, a doctor classified and sorted the wounded – only the worst cases were dealt with by us. Already after the first case I realised Doctor Jolly was one of the best surgeons I had ever worked with – and certainly one of the quickest. Long before he had finished with the first case, a second ambulance drew up, and a third, and quite soon they seemed to come in droves, while the faint rumble of guns never left off.

Operating as fast as was possible for a surgeon, Jolly worked the whole afternoon, right through the night, the next day, and most of the following night as well, practically without a break. He never seemed to tire or lose his concentration, and most of the time I worked with him.

It was terrible on the front line – we were right in the midst of it. As they were coming off the ambulance, picking them up and dropping them off, we were taking on laparotomies [abdominal surgery], stomach wounds, amputations and head injuries. All they had to show us what was needed was a cross saying 'anti-tetanus' or 'morphine' – and if they weren't bad enough to need an immediate operation they were taken down the second line of evacuation. Then they'd go on to the third. But we operated on the most urgent. I could get a tray and table – you could raise or lower them, put a cloth on them, get a box with complete trephines, for head injuries and complete amputations – metal boxes with all the necessary operating instruments. We had three tables going with the other surgeon who helped, and there were Spanish nurses – not that they knew a thing, but they soon learnt how to do things. We showed them how to take things out – 'Don't touch them with your hands, use this equipment, cover them, give them to the doctor.' We used morphine and drips, but we were always running out. It was very, very difficult. Most of the cases were too far gone to give them anything to put them out, and there were terrible, terrible losses. People died who should never have died.

All three operating tables had to work together, and our supply of instruments was far too limited. The moment one operation was over, I gathered the instruments, hurried to the girl outside – I'd shown her how they should be washed and put in the steriliser and brought in again for the next case. In the meantime, I was back at the operating table and making it ready for the next case. After a while, I could change over so quickly that, less than five minutes after a case was taken off, the operating table was prepared for the next.

In the intervals we had food brought into the operating theatre – chunks of bread and bully beef, and black coffee, and snatched a few bites when we could. Nor did we bother much about the rule of no smoking in operating theatres – we quickly smoked cigarettes in the doorway while waiting for our instruments. Coffee and cigarettes helped, but, after a time, what with the din and the endless flow of wounded, I thought I would go crazy through lack of sleep and overwork.

Once, just as we were thinking of finishing, but still had several cases to deal with, we heard the loud drone of planes, and at once our lights, including the emergency light, went out. Before we could move, there were shattering crashes quite close, and the sound of falling glass. The next minute there were unearthly shrieks from outside and the sound of people running. Our doors were open, and, before we knew what was going on, there was a wild stampede in the darkness. Civilians were rushing into our hospital, which was already full of our own wounded. The air was full of shrieking and moaning.

A man collided with me and, as I put out my hand to push him off, my fingers touched his hair and came off all sticky. I had pushed him into a chair and, when the lights came on again, I saw that he was an old man, and half the flesh of his face was blown off. Other men and women were in a pitiful state, being helped into the hospital by their friends, some gashed by shrapnel, others with legs and arms half blown off, half-naked and bleeding women who'd been blown out of their clothes.

At this time we were attached to the American unit – nothing to do with the British. I never came into contact with the British, who were supposed to be busy on that front. How busy I don't know, but they couldn't have been as busy as we were. We were very, very busy, and we never saw any English in my unit.

We got a wonderful van from the Americans. At the back there was complete sterilising equipment for instruments and one for gowns and sheets, then, on the side, all the instruments for head cases and amputations, and on the other side was all the linen required – it was wonderful. The Americans knew how to do things. The British used to give us things, but in dribs and drabs – but never enough, really.

I sometimes walked across the square and looked at the bomb-wrecked buildings. It made me think of London, with its miles of overcrowded, jerry-built slums. What chance would these overcrowded people have in air raids? The rich in the West End and Kensington would no doubt escape in their cars, but the East End would be a death trap. But then I thought, if the Fascists in Spain were beaten, there wouldn't be any danger of air raids over London. I never ceased to believe this, all the time I was in Spain. Spain was a warning of what would happen to all of us. If we let Spain go, then it would be our fate, too, to go to war.

On one occasion I came in contact with a doctor in the English unit. I'd had a very tiring time following a really hard bombing, and we'd just finished in the early hours of the morning. The sun was shining and I thought I'd go round to the square – there was a little coffee shop and some English ambulance drivers used to gather there. Further up was another shop where people used to sit outside. I passed the main Madrid–Valencia road and turned into a cobbled square where there was the gasoline station where lorries were refuelling.

As I passed the guard, the doctor called out to me, and, because he could speak English, I went over and sat down near him. It was very hot; there were a number of small children playing near the mules and carts. I had been sitting for about two minutes when, without warning – not even the peal of church bells – there were terrific crashes, my hand automatically flew up to my ears, my chair went from under me and I was on the floor. At once there was another terrific explosion, masonry and bricks were falling everywhere, and clouds of dust swirling so that nothing could be seen for a moment except a blaze of flames. Then came the shrieks. For a moment I didn't know what was happening, and then realised this was an aerial bombardment, and I dashed across the road, across the bloody mess of bricks, to get to the children. By this time the petrol station was a sheet of flames, and I almost fell on top of a small child lying on the ground, covered with debris. It was awful, and I shall never forget it. As I picked the child up, it seemed to regain consciousness and struggled in my arms, and I had to hold it tightly, which was difficult because one leg was only hanging on by a sinew. For one moment I stood with the child in my arms, horror-struck. My legs were so weak I couldn't move. One of the medical people saw me struggling with the child and took it from me and carried it to the hospital. It was sickening. But what happened to all the other people, and the mules and the fuel? It was just a big flash. It must have been a terrific bomb – they were trying to hit the line between Madrid and Valencia. It was that day when I first met the doctor from the English unit, Doctor Alex Tudor-Hart, and he took me to his hospital. He said I couldn't go back to my hospital, that I'd better stay. He tried to keep me there – but I knew I had to go back.

We had a man come round – a relative of one of the people who was killed when the bomb went off. We used to mother him and see that his things were ready for him after a day's work. He had had a job at one time as a porter, overseeing the prevention of typhoid, and he used to go round and was very suspicious of the water. We never had typhoid antitoxins – we were never inoculated against it. It should have been done in London really before coming out to Spain.

I set out with a medical unit to set up another first hospital of evacuation near the Jarama River. It was the end of February and the weather in this part of Spain was bitterly cold. Perales, where we stopped, was only a small, poor village, built round a large, empty, cobbled square. Continuing some way beyond the village, we stopped outside the courtyard of a rough stone building, rather like a barn, standing in a dell, surrounded by trees. The yard was full of slush and mud, open to cold winds coming over the low hills, beyond which lay the front.

There was no electric light, which we had to rig up from our own petrol motor. Nor was water laid on – it was brought to us daily by cart in huge water urns, and when the carts came we filled every pot and jar and bottle in the place to last out the day. It was not considered good drinking water, and we were never supposed to drink it unboiled – but when instruments were waiting to be sterilised and cases arriving continuously, no one had time for such luxuries as boiling drinking water. We took the risk of getting typhoid or enteritis, because there was no time to do anything else.

The first day at our post was fairly quiet and we had time to take a look around in the cold afternoon light. But early the next morning the guns began to fire, sounding terribly close. In the evening the first cases started to arrive. We worked in one spell until about 5.30 in the morning, and for the next two weeks or more we lived in a nightmare. My unit was a Spanish one, with three Spanish surgeons and one or two French nurses – and we were pretty poorly equipped. Already, during the first night, wounded men were being brought in faster than we could deal with them, and, instead of slackening, their number only increased. By the second day, we were flooded with wounded men.

It was ghastly. Inside the operating theatre we had no heating except a gasoline stove, and sometimes it was so cold I would be glad to be in a room crammed full of people to share their bodily heat. I was working as anaesthetist, assistant surgeon and theatre nurse. I had to decide which case was the most urgent for operation, and then at once set up tables for instruments. Meanwhile, the casualty was placed on the operating table and I first sent him off with ethyl chloride, keeping my hand over the mask to prevent it from flaking in the cold, and then started him on ether. When he was well under, I would hand over to an orderly, showing him how to keep the man's chin well forwards, so that the tongue wouldn't fall back, and how to regulate the ether flow. Then I would rush to scrub up and be ready to assist the surgeon, holding the ligatures or dealing with the swabs. The rate we worked, many items must have been sewn up inside the patients.

The smell of ether never left me, and often in the theatre I was sure I would pass out, standing up, long before the patient. Sometimes I felt so tired I really thought I couldn't go on – then we would stop and have a Spanish cigarette and some black coffee and begin again. At times I used to stumble out for air, and, as I tried to get out, I would keep tripping over bodies – some dead and some wounded. That and the cries of the wounded for *'agua'* always made us go on. I don't know where our energy came from.

At the Battle of Jarama many were slaughtered, and it was horrific. There were heavy losses. It should never have happened – what was needed was someone who had some knowledge of warfare. They were all youngsters – inexperienced – and a lot of lives were lost that shouldn't have been. We worked very hard in Jarama – Langer, Goryan and few more wonderful people. We were involved in that battle for the whole session, until we had time to retire. Whoever was going to go on the offensive, you were prepared. You got all your stuff ready for a big onslaught, whichever side was attacking. Sometimes it might be that we were going to be attacked so we got prepared, then when it started you would be ready. And it would be horrific – casualties on both sides – and it would last for quite a few days. Then there'd be a gradual clearing off and things would settle down and you'd try to reorganise yourself. Then there'd be a counter-attack, and you'd have to be ready for that. Many a time I would take the ambulance and go to Madrid to replenish some of our equipment and get ready for a counter-attack, whoever did it, whether it be us or the other side, so you weren't allowed out of the compound for long. But war is a lot of suffering for the civilians, too, especially in one place. It was hell – we had the whole population rushing screaming into our hospital. You'd put your hand out to try and stop them – but they were bleeding and crushed. I think the whole of the village was on fire.

Among strangers in Perales, with the little Spanish I had learnt, it was difficult for me to make myself understood. I was merely '*Camarada* [Comrade] Penny'. It was a young Spanish lad, the only one who could sometimes interpret a few sentences, who first called me 'English Penny'. First it was a joke, then the name stuck. Soon I was 'English Penny' wherever I went in Spain.

I found the Spaniards were much less sensitive to pain. In operations in England we would always give chloroform and they were performed under local anaesthetic. Once I had a fierce quarrel with one of our doctors – a Catalan. A man had been brought in with his arm almost severed, hanging on only by shreds of muscle and tendons, and I was just preparing the anaesthetic mask when this Catalan surgeon walked round the table and looked down. And the next moment, with one quick movement, he had slashed the arm right off, and the man let out a piercing scream. I was livid, but the surgeon tried to explain that it was only a matter of a second. Other cases were waiting and in this way time had been gained. I said it was wicked to give the man such a shock. It was bad enough for him to have his arm hanging on by shreds, but to have it suddenly gone was too much.

One night, very late, I went out into the yard, where wounded men were still lying, attended only by Spanish orderlies – and all of these were asleep. I looked round to see what I could do, and some of the men seemed thirsty so I gave them water. Going back to the entrance, I suddenly stumbled over a man I hadn't noticed and almost fell on top of him. I said in Spanish, 'Sorry, *camarada*.' He didn't answer – or move at all – and I suddenly realised that my hand was resting on his face and that it was cold as stone. It must have been many hours ago that he had died. When I regained my balance I found I was shaking; very quickly I walked through the dark to the hospital door, thinking of the touch of my hand on the dead man, and, just as I opened it, a hand touched my shoulder. I went ice-cold. I imagined the dead man had got up and was touching me. I screamed and let the water jug fall with a clatter – then discovered it was only the guard on duty who was standing behind me. He had made coffee and was going to give me some – I collapsed into the nearest chair, shaking all over.

It seemed to have been quiet for a few days, and our counter-attack had definitely gained ground, and it was said that another Fascist attack on Madrid had failed. When this was confirmed, we packed up and returned to Tarancón. The little town was full of military. In spite of our heavy casualties, the general feeling was cheerful, and everyone said the International Brigades had again saved Madrid. For a few days we were able to rest, but I found I had almost lost the habit of sleep. In spite of the cheerful atmosphere I couldn't help thinking of the casualties – of the men dying in our yard.

I was moved to the international hospital at the little town of Colmenar Viejo, where I met Una Wilson, a New Zealander, very tall and blonde, and May Macfarlane, an Australian, small, dark, with tortoiseshell glasses, both of them experienced nurses. I got to be very friendly with them; then there was Dumont, very good-looking, Belgian, fond of music –

very arrogant but a very brilliant young surgeon. I liked working with him; I knew just what he wanted – didn't have to stop. Then there was Langer, who used to go round all the field hospitals to see what they wanted.

Then, about two weeks after arriving at Colmenar Viejo, I began to feel unwell, suffering from headaches and tiredness, but Una Wilson was ill for a spell and May Macfarlane was very run down, so I kept on working, putting my troubles down to overwork and lack of good food. For months now we had been living on bread, beans, occasional bully beef and black coffee. One day I had such a bad headache that I could not keep my head up. I took a dessert spoonful of aspirin and lay down, and the pain went – but that night I felt ill again and found myself coughing and restless. When Una asked what the matter was, I said I was so tired I couldn't sleep. Dr Dumont came, said I had a *grippe* [flu] and was to stay in bed. Next morning I still had the headache. Dumont came up, looked at me and said he would fetch a thermometer. Something urgent must have delayed him – anyway, he never came, and, as I lay there waiting for him, my headache became so acute I couldn't bear it. The room started going round and round, and I remembered nothing more. I just felt I couldn't go on. I was just walking and walking – and I woke up hearing someone was calling me: 'Penny, Penny!' It was May Macfarlane, and they had found me walking outside the compound in my bare feet, quite delirious, and one of the guards brought me back.

I later learnt that when I was brought inside Dr Dumont

had taken me straight to his room. Langer came to look at me and at first glance had said, 'Typhoid'. Una Wilson and May Macfarlane had taken it in turns to nurse me. If it hadn't been for them I'd have been in the lap of the gods, but they nursed me. I had gone straight into a coma, which meant I was already in the third week of the illness, and had passed through the first stages while up on my feet and still working. I remained in bed over a month altogether, and I suppose in a way I was lucky to pull through, because my crisis had lasted a week, and later, when a number of English boys were passing through, they were amazed to see me. They had heard quite definitely I had died.

I felt washed out after the typhoid – tired and physically depressed. Because there was no urgent work, Langer suggested I should take a short leave to go to England. And I agreed because I'd be able to bring back some urgently needed instruments.

So I went home for a while, and, while I was back, I spoke to people. One person yelled out in some big hall, 'Spain is red.'

And I said, 'Yes, it is red, it's red with blood. My arms are filled with it, right up to my sleeves. Yes, it's red.'

I'll always remember that. I don't know who it was who called out, but I'll always remember that whoever it was who organised this meeting said that my response was the *pièce de résistance* – the highlight of the evening. I was wearing a new hat, and it was so hot – there was a lovely brim on this new hat, and I was so proud of it. As I went on the platform, it was so jolly hot that I took my hat off – and they thought that was wonderful.

Being in England felt like being in a foreign country. At first I couldn't get used to people's purposeless lives – the drab look of London. People seemed to me unreal – not interested in anything and never thinking beyond the petty details of their own lives. I spoke at a series of meetings arranged by the Spanish Medical Aid Committee, and, though I had no experience of public speaking, I think I managed to bring home to people what was happening out in Spain. The best meetings, I thought, were those in the East End and in poor, working-class districts. All in all, I collected quite a lot of money and was going back with a good collection of new surgical instruments – some bought, some donated from hospitals. But I knew what a small drop in the ocean this was, and how even people who were sympathetic had not really understood. They might feel sorry about Spain, but above all they wanted England to be kept out of it.

Returning, we travelled through Madrid in the dusk, in a long chain of ambulances, led by a huge American motor van in which most of our mobile equipment was stored. It was an eerie scene. Madrid seemed dead. The streets were empty and silent except for us and the troop convoys we passed, all moving in the same direction with artillery and a few tanks. I soon realised it was always the same story with us – lorries full of infantry moving against the mechanised Fascist armies.

Near midday we arrived at Hoyo de Manzanares, where we were to stay. This was entirely different Spanish country from the poor market towns such as Tarancón, Perales or Colmenar. It must have been one of Madrid's wealthiest and smartest summer resorts. It had large villas with wonderful gardens full of flowers, still in good order, sunshine everywhere and yet with invigorating air, green fields and, at the back, the wonderful sight of the snow-capped sierras.

Hoyo de Manzanares hospital was set aside for minor surgical cases, while our first hospital for treatment and evacuation of serious cases was a large house called La Solana at Torrelodones, a place between two hills on the junction of the roads from Madrid to El Escorial and to Brunete. It was an old house – not very large – but what pleased me was that there was a small room at the top, just large enough for two beds, which May Macfarlane and I took for ourselves, so that we wouldn't have to sleep on cold stretchers stiff with caked blood.

That evening and night, 5 July 1937, troops moved up to the attack scheduled for the following day, tramping quietly past our building and singing while they marched. Wine and cigarettes had been distributed and all the different international battalions as they marched past sang their own national songs. It was marvellous, the tramp-tramp and the sound of soft singing through the night, not a light showing – a deep, emotional experience. I wondered what would happen to all these men, and, even while hoping for victory, I had to ask myself, how many casualties?

I thought I would get some rest and lay down in my sleeping bag and fell asleep. Suddenly I heard a voice – 'Penny!

Penny!' – and somebody was shaking me. There were cases waiting in the theatre. I scrambled up and saw it was hardly daylight yet. I couldn't see any ambulances and couldn't understand it, but when I got to the theatre I found the cases were Spanish children who had discovered hand grenades in Torrelodones and exploded them. One kid had facial injuries and another poor mite had both hands blown off – it would go through life like this, as a lasting memory of the civil war, if it survived. We dealt with them as best we could and sent them back to the village. Before we had finished, the sun had appeared; a roar of guns told us the attack had started, and soon guns were going off all round, Fascist planes dropping bombs unpleasantly close – so close that our whole house shook with the explosions.

On the first day, our troops had taken Villanueva de la Cañada; on the second they stormed Brunete, an important Fascist town, and they were still advancing. Everyone was in jubilant spirits the night after the capture of Brunete. At the hospital everyone was so cheerful that, tired as we were after two days' almost uninterrupted work, we decided to have a party round one of the wine barrels brought from Brunete. It was a midnight party in the dark, warm fields, and I can remember it well. Naturally, we showed no lights, and we were sitting or lying around in the dark, singing Spanish and international songs, very softly. Then I looked up at the sky, which was full of stars, and suddenly I saw something and said, 'What's that glittering up there?' Somebody laughed and said it was only the telephone wires, but the next moment we saw a searchlight shoot up, then a second, and a few more. They were like silver spears in the sky, and there, not far away, we saw a Fascist plane, flying low, which had crept in on the sly, and was now dodging desperately to get away. The lights lost him – found him again – but couldn't hold him, and then he was too far away and had escaped unhurt.

The capture of Brunete had been a quick success, but the Fascist army must have rushed up new troops because fighting raged day after day over the same few miles of ground. Every day we worked in the hospital, and, though we were never as badly caught for organisation as on the Jarama, the constant flow of ambulances and wounded gave us little respite.

We didn't know much about what was going on. It was kept from us, really. We used to try to guess because we had people coming through with bits of gossip, and you put them together, but I think Goryan was worried about what was happening – because he was the one who was doing all the outside organising. They didn't let us know much, but we knew generally what was going on, and which area was getting ready to move off and at what time. You were never told where you were going, but you just had to be ready.

While we were at La Solana, there was a terrible time when we lost the three doctors – my best friends, really. These doctors, very well-known surgeons, went to the front to cheer the men up because it was quiet and they were bored. Coming back they got a direct hit, so all these people I knew so well were killed outright. That upset me very much. I took a long time to get over that.

The heat was terrific, and in the theatre it brought millions of flies. They settled on the wounds and instruments and everything! We had no Flit, so I used to spray them with ethyl chloride.

Day after day we only finished operating in the early hours of the morning, with only a few hours' rest before the next spell. The worst was the bombings – we got no peace from the air because the Fascists knew how much the destruction of a hospital would disorganise us.

Once I went down to the little river at the back of us and took off my shoes and waded in the water between the boulders to relieve my feet. On the other side of the stream some peasants were guarding their cattle. It often happened in Spain that peasants would stay almost on the battlefield rather than lose their only possessions. Suddenly I saw planes come low over the horizon. They were gliding down silently, and, as I thought I could see red markings on the wings, I believed them to be our planes – but the next minute I heard the splatter of machine guns and realised they were camouflaged Fascist planes. Right along the little valley they flew low, machine-gunning everybody and everything. I flung myself down flat among the boulders, heard the ping of bullets striking stone all around, saw the shadows pass, and, when I looked up, saw the planes already well away. There were the cattle kicking on the ground, two peasants apparently wounded and a third shouting frantically and waving his arm. I ran as fast as I could to give help.

Because the battle had lasted so much longer than expected,

we were fearfully short of supplies. Time and again I gave an anaesthetist a bottle of ether saying, 'This is the last we have.' Once, we were left in the dark – the main lights were cut off, and our own motor failed us while three operations were in progress. Two surgeons had the use of the only two torches in the place. The third surgeon had just begun sewing up and I held my cigarette lighter for him.

Again it was decided that I should go back to England and bring back much-needed supplies. In England the novelty of the Spanish war had worn off and everyone was much less interested, thinking only of their summer holidays or ordinary office routine. When I thought of the brave men who had died at Brunete, fighting for freedom – for English freedom, too – I felt English people didn't care and wouldn't think, and it made me bitter. England seemed to me unreal and insane. Either England or Spain was unreal, and it was not Spain.

Returning to Spain, I met May Macfarlane on the way back and we went into Albacete. It was midnight when I arrived, and, as always in this place, it was cold and raining hard, and I felt my usual 'Albacete gloom and depression' steal over me.

Langer had been promoted and was now chief medical organiser. We found him in his office – a small room containing a bed and desk, some files and two telephones, on the walls a few anti-Fascist posters. Everything was clean and tidy. As soon as he greeted us, thoughts of England faded from my mind and I felt back in my real place and at my real work.

Langer was in a terrible way, pacing up and down, trying to think out what to do, and he said, 'Thank God you've arrived.'

I said, 'What?'

'You've had fever experience, haven't you?'

'Yes,' I said, 'I trained as a fever nurse.'

'Good, I'm going to send you and a medical officer to the Garibaldis.'

I said, 'Who are the Garibaldis?'

They were Italians, and I didn't know a word of Italian.

'It's all right, you're going as their medical officer.'

There was typhoid on the Aragón Front, where men were going down with it like flies, and, just before we arrived, another call had come through from the Garibaldi Battalion – based at Quintanar de la República, fifty kilometres away – saying that they had scarlet fever and asking for a doctor. The Garibaldis' doctor had gone down with typhoid – but the whole of this troop was ready to go to the front, in the north, to relieve their comrades there. When their doctor went sick, they had no one. So I went.

A tumbledown old ambulance arrived, with a very disagreeable little boy for the driver – with whom we became great friends afterwards – and we set off into the unknown. It was a terrible experience, them not knowing a word of English, and it was only the *commandante*, the political commissar, who was in charge. He was away when I first arrived, late at night, with it pouring with rain. I got out of the ambulance, gathered a bundle of blankets and gowns from the back, then we had to cross an open space across ruts so deep we sank almost knee-deep in soft mud. I hadn't even brought my top boots, not knowing what the place was like. We clambered up the side of the road and arrived in front of a big, dark building, almost on the main road. This was the hospital.

We tried banging on the door from the road, but it was late at night and we couldn't get an answer. Finally, bang, bang, bang and this little slot came undone. *'Nada! Mañana.'* The door was shut again. Bang, bang, bang. Then finally the door opened with a guard looking at us pointing a revolver. I said 'Albacete'. That was all I could say – 'Albacete' – and he put down his gun and opened the door into the hospital – that's what it was. I went in and it was a terrible place. It was a beautiful building but it was in a fearful state, and the smell was dreadful. Going round the beds I saw one man who looked terribly ill, went up to him and realised it was typhoid. I only had to look at him. I started working immediately, ordering things about, much to the reluctance of the man who opened the door. We woke up the people upstairs who were supposed to be on duty looking after the patients – there was no order at all. My first patient was the typhoid case – desperately ill – but I managed to get him out. Whether he lived or not after he was moved I don't know, but that was one case, then there was all the business of reorganising. I didn't know what I was in for.

Inside, the whole ward was terribly overcrowded. The beds were so close there was only room to shuffle – not walk – between them. Practically none of the men had pillows, but were sleeping on bundles of their clothes. Everything was untidy – beds and floors littered with breadcrumbs, one or two glasses of half-drunk wine standing about, chamber pots under beds full to overflowing. All the windows were shut tight and the stench was awful.

It was very, very difficult to take that great responsibility for what might happen – knowing that I might be held to account for what I did. I just prayed to the gods for strength. At three o'clock the next morning I was dead tired and hungry, and thought, 'What shall I do?' But I took some wine, fell asleep – I don't know for how long – and when I woke up I was all right. Apparently the political commissar was still away, but he would be back soon. I went to see the next in command and I told him what was happening and all the things that must be done to prevent typhoid. He listened but all he could say that I understood was '*sí, sí, sí*', so I requested an interpreter when the next train came, and Langer promised me he would send one. In fact, he sent me two, both very good men. At last I brought some order to bear, and we started making progress. I got people from the village to work, mending and so on.

To wipe out the scarlet fever epidemic I would have to fumigate all dwellings and sleeping quarters; all clothing and articles capable of carrying infection had to be disinfected. I needed new quarters for one whole company – and I took over a church. It was empty, its trimmings and trappings all removed to safe storage. The commander of the company of workers at the base was a tall, boyish-looking Spaniard – very polite – and he agreed to see that sufficient beds were prepared for a company, and I would order mattresses from Albacete. He told me that it had been difficult to get more than a few men to turn up for baths, which wasn't surprising because the showers had been ice-cold, and even then not running regularly. I gave orders for warm showers to be fixed up, by however temporary an arrangement. By the next day, during disinfection, every man was to have a warm shower bath. The tall Spaniard promised it would be done, one way or another.

The men of one company were assembled, they stripped in one room, leaving boots, belts and other leather articles in one corner, their clothes in a second, and their personal belongings, done up in little marked cloth bundles, in a third. Then everything was gathered together and disinfected. The men, in the meantime, entered the shower place, where they were thoroughly scrubbed, and any sores and cuts dressed with sulphur ointment. Then, wearing only towels around their middles, they filed in batches of five into my room to be examined. Some of them were self-conscious, though I had hardly time to notice individuals.

It was amazing what was achieved in such a short time. And then Roberto Vincenzi came. Everyone spoke in awe of him, and I wondered who he could be that they seemed in such awe. When he arrived, he seemed to me to be just a very, very good-looking man. He spoke very good English. It turned out we got on very well. He loved me, I think, Roberto – and he helped me quite a lot.

For some two weeks, each of my days was a repetition of the last, till in the end the entire battalion of more than six hundred men and officers had passed through the disinfecting process. When Langer came to see me after about two weeks, he was amazed. He said one could smell the disinfectant even before approaching the village, and that the general condition of the barracks was as good as any he had seen.

When I think how I inoculated those men, God, they were tough guys, they really were tough guys. But a lot of them used to swing the lead – but I got on very well with them and I was treated quite well for being a woman among them. I used to have my meals with them – not that I liked the Spanish food – but I never drank their wines. I didn't drink with them – there was plenty of talk about what wonderful wines they made, but I never drank.

My small hospital was well occupied. I had plenty of minor doctor's work – the soldiers came to me particularly when pieces of shrapnel or bone from earlier wounds were working themselves out. I would give a local anaesthetic and remove the foreign body myself. Besides, the hospital being in charge of the sanitary and medical arrangements of the barracks gave me a full day's work. I regularly inspected the soldiers' beds, the kitchens and dining rooms. As I passed through, accompanied by my escorts, the soldiers had to hold out utensils and drinking mugs for my inspection. I saw to it that everything, particularly sanitary arrangements, remained in perfect order.

Quintanar was a bleak village. The place swarmed with ragged, barefoot children. In the afternoons I had arranged a regular consultation for civilians, mostly attended by mothers with children who had various ailments or injuries. I had cuts and injured heads aplenty, and soon became quite a dab hand at stitching. It was hard to see how people lived in such squalor, poverty and disease, chiefly through their own ignorance. Even before the war, many of the children had been dreadfully undernourished, but the war had made food conditions worse, and it was heartbreaking to tell mothers there was nothing wrong with their children except lack of food. I could issue medicines, tonics and bandages, and for a few special cases among the children I slipped in milk rations from our store of supplies from Albacete – strictly against war regulations, but I couldn't help myself. At first the peasants regarded me rather suspiciously, but, after a time, when they saw my work they took to me and I was often invited round to their houses, where once or twice a chicken was triumphantly produced from a secret hiding place and roasted for dinner.

After discussion with Langer it was decided that the whole population must be inoculated against typhoid, as the only means to prevent a serious epidemic. Supplies of TAB serum arrived for me from Albacete, but, to my dismay, not in small ampoules of 0.5cc injections, but in big 100cc bottles of highly concentrated serum. I knew what giving too strong an injection of typhoid serum might mean, and in calculating the exact doses I was badly handicapped by my fatal weakness in arithmetic. At last, however, after nearly breaking my head over the calculations, I got the measurements pat. I pre-pared a supply of needles, and, with the help of my orderlies, inoculated the entire civil population in two days.

When I think about it, it was only a little village but there were a lot of old people there – grannies left to look after the children – and they used to have terrible accidents. The grannies used to hold the children in their chairs by the table and they'd go off to sleep and underneath the table were these trays – they used to sift cinders in them when they did the coals, just like my mother did. The cinders would stay alight and give off heat and these people used to keep them under the table to keep them warm – but often they'd drop the child when they nodded off, so I had several accidents with burns, even though I was not supposed to attend the civilian population. I felt I was making a difference and it was a wonderful experience.

I developed a cough which bothered me as I went about my work, and in no time I went down with flu. By this time I felt my work at Quintanar was completed, so I got in touch with Langer, asking him to let me return to my job of front-line nursing. Langer agreed, so I said goodbye to the little village of Quintanar. Back at the English villa in Valencia I found Una Wilson, Phyllis Herbert and several other English nurses, all back from the front line at Teruel. Sybil Clarke looked after us beautifully and it was heavenly to be able to sit down to afternoon tea again – we even had a few pats of real butter – and chat with English girls.

But now we seemed to be bombed day and night, no longer as an exception, but as a regular procedure. Mainly the bombers simply flew in straight lines across the town, dropping their bombs indiscriminately for the purpose of destruction and intimidation.

I came back to England again for a short break – and specifically to get medical supplies. In April 1938 I returned from leave with all the materials I had promised Goryan – drugs, needles and tinned food and English cigarettes. I was determined to get through to him – as determined as I had ever been about anything in my life. If the road was cut, I would smuggle myself in on one of the barges that slipped through at night, from a port on the French side to one in Spain. I got through and found that there was an ambulance in Barcelona about to return to Uclés, near Madrid, and the driver was as set as I on cutting through while he could. First thing next morning we started out in the ambulance, and on the way to Tarragona we came upon masses of refugees, all pouring along the coastal road in the opposite direction to us – men, women and children on foot, peasants with ox carts piled high with bedding, furniture and children. For the first time I saw a real mass flight, and I realised the extent of Spain's disaster.

It seemed to me that, in spite of people being disillusioned, a new spirit was arising. The Spanish nation was rallying, and everywhere very young men were joining the ranks and being drilled, and forming their own more and more efficient army – but I noticed another thing. Mr Chamberlain had just signed his Anglo-Italian pact, and the Spanish newspapers had a photograph of him, all full of smiles; and now among the ordinary Spanish people, who saw Italian planes come day after day over the sea to bomb them, bitter feelings were rising up against England.

A girl who worked in a big factory, who was half English, told me there had already been one or two unpleasant incidents for her – and who could blame the Spaniards? There would be little love or gratitude for England on the Fascist side either, I thought, with more Germans in control. Once or twice, as Valencia was being bombed, I thought of the bombs that would inevitably fall on London in a few years' time – on my own people. All this made me only too eager to get away to the front.

We travelled in the ambulance, towards Castellón, and then turned up into the mountains to Teruel province. It was night before we finally stopped at a rough little place, full of soldiers, where I left my materials in a barn which served as reserve store. Then we drove further up again, and at last, by then very late in the night, we stopped outside a small house. Jumping down, I saw a small oil lamp and, in its light, Goryan with three other officers in a small room almost filled with four beds. As I came in, his face lit up, and he laughed and said, '*Salud*, Penny. I knew you would come!' At last I had arrived.

The full force of German, Italian and Spanish Fascism was attacking Valencia. The Spanish Army of the Levant fought and retreated, made another stand, and again evacuated the ground – and each time we moved with them, being forced back towards Valencia and the sea. All the while, as we were driven towards Valencia, more and more Fascist planes came down over the mountains and we were bombed and machine-gunned, and scores of men were killed. We were being bombed regularly – but I wasn't frightened. The one thing was to find a place you could be safe. Up there in the mountains, I lost all count of time – we patched up the wounded soldiers who were brought down the mountain-side in an endless stream.

Franco was gaining strength but nurses were now being trained to help in the effects of the bombings so I met some of these Spanish girls, and we were operating down in a gorge in the mountains. In the winter this gorge would be rushing with water, but it was lovely spot when it was dry in summer and we used the gorge as our base. Whether we were operating or had finished operating I don't know, but what happened next was we were on the move down because we were being pushed from the mountains by Franco's bombers.

I have no recollection of what happened when we were bombed – the memory is wiped out. What I do remember is that I woke up in a barn full of wounded people, lying on my back on a stretcher, naked except for tight bandages around my chest and abdomen. A medical orderly was giving me an injection of intramuscular saline, and the pain of it had woken me. I told him to stop it. I found I hadn't a stitch on me, and all I could see were bloodstains on the bandage round my chest. Also, my right arm was in plaster. Feeling with my left hand, I sensed congealed blood round my chin and nostrils, and my ears were full of dried blood, too. I tried to talk – to say something to the orderly and tell him he was hurting me with the injection – but I was dazed and couldn't think. No Spanish words came. Eventually I asked for a blanket, which someone gave me to cover me up.

A doctor arrived and told me there had been a direct hit upon our station, and that I had sustained fractured ribs, abdominal injuries and a bruised and lacerated arm. I pointed to the blood on my chest, but he explained that this was only blood I had coughed up. The force of the explosion had caused contusion of the lungs.

I was relieved at that. I was not in much pain, but still too stunned to keep awake. During the next days I think I had regular morphine injections. I dozed, regained consciousness, lost it again. I was going to be evacuated to Benicasim. Here we were told we would be evacuated to Valencia – and there were so many wounded at the station that I realised that all Benicasim was being evacuated, too. In a dim way it floated through my mind that, if the Fascists were so near the sea, Castellón would fall too – and then Valencia. Was the war over?

It was all very disjointed and noisy, and I remember being on this journey in an open lorry with a crowd of other people, but I don't know where we were – Castellón or some place – then eventually I was put into hospital for evacuees at Benicasim, which we used as a convalescent base for the soldiers, but which was now being used to treat casualties. It was all very muddled, but I remember there were reporters everywhere. When I was moved again to Valencia, I said I wanted to go to the English unit's hospital, but they took no notice and took me to what I presume was a military hospital.

I gathered that I was very ill. After consultation with a Spanish doctor, they suggested a laparotomy – no, never, I thought – and I protested. I was not going to have an abdominal operation – not here in Spain under war conditions! I had seen too many of them. In spite of my weak condition, I was so determined in my protests that they left me. I knew if I had a laparotomy that would be the end of me.

I said I'd rather carry on with the drugs to ease the pain. The nurses were very good and gradually things settled down – but the English got to know about me through a reporter who had heard that an English nurse had been injured.

Later I felt I was getting better – at least I thought so. My ribs were healing, along with the rather curious cuts on my stomach, and I didn't see why I should not recover rapidly. The first time there was an air raid I promptly tried to get up, which was stupid of me. I succeeded in getting to the stairs, then fell down and was badly bruised.

There was room for only one thought and one deter-mination in my mind – I must get better. I don't know now why I didn't try to find out more what the matter with me was. I think I was still suffering from the shock of being injured. These were nightmare days – we had terrific aerial bombardments, shaking the whole neighbourhood of the port. One night the planes passed over us in direct line and, though their bombs missed us, the house next to us was smashed. Another group of people sheltering on the beach were mangled by the explosion, and a second bomb wiped out a gun and crew not a hundred yards away, also on the beach. The force of the explosions blew out all our windows, and plaster fell in such lumps that for a moment the whole building seemed about to collapse. There was a fearful mess on the beach – a dozen people were dead. One woman had a leg blown clean off, and I remember wandering erratically across the sands, trying to find that leg – I don't know why.

I was to be evacuated with a group leaving on a British warship. Because the British consul decided Valencia was too unsafe, I was taken by ambulance to Gandía, a small port on the other side of Alicante in the vine-growing country, which I now glimpsed for the first time. At Gandía I was the last of the wounded to be ferried out to the ship in a speedboat. A smart British naval officer was in charge. He smiled at me and said, 'Are you all right?' He looked so calm and well-dressed; I realised I had not seen a man like him for months.

The *Sussex* seemed so spick and span – clean decks, polished metalwork and guns – and the British officers looked neat and well-shaven. There was tea, good food, cigarettes and quiet – another world from the one I had left. They took us as far as Marseilles, and they were very good to me – especially the surgeon on the ship. At Marseilles they had apparently been waiting for me all day with an ambulance at the airport, so when I arrived they flew me back and took me straight to the New End Hospital, where I received very good attention.

I remained in hospital for what seemed a long, long time. I had developed peritonitis, but I was too weak to be operated on. I was growing weaker, which was causing some anxiety, and my mother was notified. But my obsession was 'I must go back to Spain', and the thought never quite left me. I never doubted that I should pull through – it seemed absurd to escape death in Spain, only to die immediately afterwards in a Hampstead hospital. Yet, once I was over the crisis, I could not get better. The noise of any aeroplane overhead, and the shooting from the Territorial Army machine-gun range nearby, disturbed me terribly, especially when I was not quite conscious. It reminded me of Spain, and with the rat-tat-tat and low zooming of planes, I grew frantic. Every sound, every bullet fired, seemed directed against my head. I felt I could not cope with it any more – even the noise of people walking through the ward became too much for me.

What I needed was quiet and rest and green fields, but the hospital authorities would not let me go, and when I threatened to discharge myself, and said I would not remain any longer – not another hour – Lady Hastings, the chair of Spanish Medical Aid, and one of the doctors were hurriedly brought to me.

Eventually they rang up nursing homes, one after another, and the first one they found with a vacancy was a Catholic nursing home nearby at St John's Wood, and I went there the same afternoon. Peace. Peace at last. I stayed there a week – which cost ten guineas. Of course, I had no right to such luxury, which I don't suppose I'll ever need again – but it was a heavenly week, and I think helped me turn the corner.

Later I went down to Hastings, to stay quietly with friends

at a small place in the country. How wonderful to be resting peacefully in the country – to see trees and a green garden! By now, the conditions in Spain, along with my illness, had reduced me to a mere skeleton. My weight was under six stone, but at Hastings I was lucky with the weather. I lay in the sun, or slept quietly in my room. At the end of the first two weeks I had put on eight pounds in weight; during the third week I gained another eight pounds. Before the end of one month, I was already trying to play some gentle tennis.

The shrapnel injuries didn't worry me any more, but still I was not as strong as I thought. I took on a short temporary hospital job early in September – and that was queer enough, with its discipline – but I found the work exhausting, and on the third day I fainted. I was really not fit for any work. Now at last I knew that I could not return to Spain – I was in no state of health to be useful.

During the war one felt a lot of emotions. There were people you knew and loved, and there were one or two people I really was very upset over, but you shouldn't let your emotions overcome you. That's the thing in nursing – you should never let your emotions overcome you because it ruins you for work. But many a time I lost a very, very good friend – but that's life. Those people were all so very precious – because life itself is precious. But for me it was a wonderful experience. I met so many people.

You might hear people talking on the wireless now – they think they know what it's about – but they don't know. It's very difficult to correlate all the impressions together and get an exact picture; it's all very disjointed, even people's different personalities. Some people changed rapidly after you'd known them for a bit – and some you'd get disappointed in. When I met Mick I told him about Roberto. I had grown very fond of him, and he was very good to his people. He had always taken care of me and was my mentor – and he used to escort me, as there were some very tough guys around, and women were very few, so I had to be protected. Roberto was very strict and very good-looking, and he took complete charge looking after me. When I married Mick I told him that Roberto was really in love with me – but assured him that I wasn't in love with Roberto: we were from two different countries and he spoke a different language which I didn't understand. But I knew what his inner thoughts were – and he really protected me. I'd heard that Franco had overrun the place, and I didn't know if Roberto had been killed or what had happened to him, so Mick tried to make enquiries through the embassies and went out of his way to see if he could do something to help – and he found where he was in France, in a concentration camp. We wrote to him and got letters back from him. I told him I was married and he told me how he loved me; Mick wrote to him and sent him parcels – cigarettes and so on. We tried to go and see him, but, by the time we went, he'd gone. Mick knew all about him – but that was the end of it. I can only presume he was taken out and shot when Hitler marched into France.

You used to think that if you're going to get hit, it happens so fast that you don't feel it – and that's what I used to tell people. It happens so quickly that you don't feel it. Under bombardment, you were trying to think of the other people who were being scared stiff, especially children and old people. When the town that was bombed, and they all came rushing into our hospital, I'll always remember putting a hand out to stop them and coming up against bits and pieces of flesh. You can't imagine – you just can't picture it.

I was standing somewhere on my own, high up on a veranda of some sort, when I heard about the bombing of Guernica. I didn't know what to think about it. I couldn't imagine it – the terrible, terrible things that happened – that people could do it. I later saw Picasso's painting of Guernica in a gallery – I don't think my mind would let me dwell on it. It's no use letting your mind do that, because otherwise you wouldn't be normal. I made good friends, and I lost good friends, but I have many good memories. At first I used to have little nightmares, but Mick, my husband, was wonderful. He'd say, 'It's all right, Pen Pen.' He said before he died – 'I'll never leave you' – and he hasn't left me. But I remember all those people who died – all those people you cradled in your arms. You didn't have much time to spare for them, but you would find just a minute or so.

War is a terrible thing – I think it's the worst thing that can happen. Such a lot of needless slaughter and misery. People don't realise what trouble they're making when they make big speeches – but that's life.

I've had a good life. I've been very lucky. I've met the right people who put me on the right road. I could have gone on the other path. Much as I wanted children it wasn't my luck to have them. I came from a household and a background where life didn't matter very much – children were being born endlessly and there was suffering.

Then I think back to the fever hospitals – thank God, you don't have them now – and I recall picking up one kiddie who had scarlet fever. He was only a tiny little thing. All I could do was pick him up from his cot and hug him.

There was a time in Spain when we thought we'd had it – in El Escorial. I didn't think we were going to make it because we were outnumbered – or at least, I thought we were. We'd lost a lot of our people and here we were, at El Escorial – the palace of the kings – a beautiful place. Everything weighed against us, but it was amazing how things turned. Something turned the tide – perhaps it was the beauty of the place. It must have appealed to people's senses – to avoid destroying a place like that.

Now, when I go back to Spain they're not interested, really. But time heals all, and time goes on and you can't live in the past. You have to go on. The experience is there, although it recedes into the background and people don't want to hear any more. They've had enough and that's that – let sleeping dogs lie.

I'd do it all again. There were many horrors. No doubt it was a bad thing, but it was worth it if something good came out of it at the end.

JACK JONES

Born 29 March 1913 in Garston, Liverpool
Died 21 April 2009 in London

I lived in York Street, Garston, in the south end of Liverpool, a long street of poor and mean two-up, two-down terraced houses, generally in a decaying state. They'd been built some time in the nineteenth century – obviously with the minimum of cost – to house labour for the nearby factories and docks. The houses were infested with rats, mice, cockroaches and bugs. Our rent was five shillings a week, and even that was exorbitant!

There was no gas or electricity, so we had a paraffin lamp downstairs, but otherwise we used candles. I was the youngest of five children, and my three brothers and I slept in one of the two bedrooms – and when we were very young, we were all in one bed. None of the houses in the street had an inside lavatory or a bathroom – we bathed in a tin bath once a week, and that wasn't easy as the water had to be heated on our single coal fire. Every morning a lad would trundle a metal barrel on wheels round the street, shouting, 'Lant!' (which meant urine) for use in the pickling process in the local copper works. The women would go out and empty the contents of their chamber pots into the barrel.

Sometimes my friends and I would attempt an invasion of the shipyard or the copper works, only to be pushed back to the gates. There we would stand until the men came out at the end of the afternoon shift. We'd call out, 'Any bread left, mister?' and occasionally we'd be rewarded with a sandwich or two, left over from a man's packed dinner. The corned beef sandwiches were the best, and, if we were especially hungry, a fight might start over them.

In our school little was taught of industrial history or the background to the lives of ordinary people – or, if there was, it wasn't taught in such a way that I remember it. Although there were no formal civics courses at school, there was plenty of practical instruction outside. I remember hearing Tom Mann and Mary Bamber [the mother of Bessie Braddock, who became Liverpool's best-known MP and City Councillor] address open-air meetings, and even as children we got to know what strikes were about – and what a terrible person a 'scab' was.

The dire position of the miners was often discussed in our home, and although I couldn't really visualise what their work was like I felt a strong sympathy for them. This feeling was strengthened when one of my uncles took me to a miners' meeting in the Wigan area, where the main speaker was A J Cook, who was the leader of the Miners' Union. I was enthralled – and the miners responded to him as a great hero. He shouted out his defiance of the mine owners – he stooped, he gestured. I remember one expression he used: 'Figures can lie, and liars can figure.' He was attacking the way statistics were being used against the miners, but his words stayed with me and often came to mind when, later in life, I saw figures being unscrupulously manipulated.

During this period I remember going with my father to hear Ernie Bevin addressing a big meeting in one of the Liverpool parks. When Bevin came off the platform, I was one of a few boys who shook his hand. However, I'm afraid his speech did not impress me – I just thought he was a big, fat man.

When the General Strike began, life seemed to change completely. I read anything I could lay my hands on, especially *The British Worker*, which was the official strike bulletin, and I listened avidly to the radio. My father and brothers were all on strike, but I didn't sense any anxiety in the family – only a desire for the strike to succeed.

My elder brother was a railwayman and member of the Associated Society of Locomotive Engineers and Firemen [ASLEF], and he was actively involved with the local Council of Action. I used to help him by running messages on my bicycle, and I felt I was part of a great army. The experiences of that time had a powerful impact on my thinking, and I closely followed the events which unfolded after the General Strike.

It was round about that time that I left school, aged

fourteen, and went to work. It wasn't easy to get a job at that time in Liverpool, and there's nothing worse than the feeling of being unwanted. I wrote lots of letters and traipsed around factories until finally I found a vacancy and later got an apprenticeship. The firm was in general engineering, making components for Graysons as well as Harland and Wolff, the shipbuilding and ship-repairing firms. As was the custom, my father signed indentures for me, and the apprenticeship was supposed to last for five years. My first pay was five shillings a week, and, as I had to take sandwiches and travel by tram and overhead railway to get to work, my contribution to the household income wasn't very much.

I regularly attended my union branch meetings and was always amazed and concerned at how few members were there. Out of a branch of some hundreds, only around twenty used to attend. There is a myth that low attendance at union meetings is a present-day phenomenon – this is not the case. There were so few members that, at the second branch meeting I ever attended, I was elected branch delegate to the Liverpool Trades Council and Labour Party – I must have been the youngest delegate by far.

Trade unionism was in my blood and I tried to encourage the same enthusiasm among my workmates. On days when we weren't working I organised visits to timber berths along the Manchester Ship Canal and at nearby Widnes, to recruit the workers there into the union, and to support them in pressing for similar rates of pay to those we were getting at Garston. We succeeded in some measure, and I became the proud possessor of the TUC Tolpuddle Medal for union recruitment.

I began to question whether the members themselves were being encouraged to play a big enough part in the work of the union. Surely the union shouldn't be seen as just another insurance company. I felt there should be more meetings of members, in addition to the so-called 'statutory' branch meetings every three months, but all my efforts were opposed by officialdom. I determined to arouse more interest in union affairs by initiating educational activity in the branch, so I pressed my case for a WEA – a Workers' Educational Association – with a class to be held each Sunday evening. This sort of thing was practically unheard of, and perhaps because of that I gained the support of some influential people in the WEA, a much more respectable body than the Liverpool Labour College. Our dockers' class met on a Sunday evening in a room above the bar in one of our local pubs, and it was well attended and popular. We made sure we always finished in good time to allow at least an hour's drinking in the bar below.

Within the union and the local Labour Party I was con-tinually pressing for action against unemployment; I felt deeply that more should be done. Unemployment was beginning to fall at that time – in the early thirties it was around two million – but a huge number of people were still unemployed. I helped lead a hunger march in February 1934 to draw attention to the problem of unemployment. It was cold and the skies were grey as the forty or so marchers set out from Liverpool. We had been joined by a group of un-employed men from Belfast and luckily a couple of them had concertinas, and they kept up our spirits by playing marching tunes. It was no holiday jaunt, though. Our clothes were not of good enough quality to keep out the cold. For some, years of unemployment meant that they embarked on the march wearing just rags and tatters, and, if it wasn't for gifts of second-hand boots provided by the march organisers, they wouldn't have been able to attempt the march at all. In a number of places we slept in the workhouse, lying on the bare boards with just a rough blanket around us. Our food there consisted of rounds of bread and a hunk of cheese – we were treated no more favourably than the usual workhouse habitué, except that we were not required to work for our board.

In Manchester, accommodation for the night was provided in All Saints' Church, where the vicar was the Reverend Etienne Watts, a very left-wing Church of England clergyman. By this time, we had been joined by many more marchers from all over Lancashire and from Manchester itself. After a meal in a nearby hall, the marchers scrambled into the church. We lay down in the pews and slept as best we could, only to be awakened in the early morning by the noise of a small congregation attending a morning service. A number of marchers, not realising the reason for the disturbance, shouted abuse and used some pretty rough language. I'm afraid it caused some consternation among the devout, but they didn't protest, and soon we were on our way to London.

In the main, the marchers aroused sympathy in the public – consciences were touched, gifts of food and clothing were made and collections were well supported. In Birmingham the workers at the Co-operative Society boot factory repaired our boots for free. At Oxford, we slept in the Corn Exchange and were looked after by the students. I was given a pair of Oxford bags [trousers] by one student, and I'm sure others did equally well.

In London I was among only a few hundred out of the two thousand who managed to gain admission to the Central Lobby. It was packed, but in the middle of the throng I saw a distinguished looking man who, I was told, was Dingle Foot – then a Liberal MP. I took my group over and we surrounded him, urging our point of view. He was visibly shaken by the examples of hardship we cited, caused by the means test, and the poverty caused by the low rates of unemployment benefit. 'How the hell can a family live on fifteen shillings and thruppence a week for the man, eight shillings for the wife, and two shillings for a child?' we asked him. He agreed to do all he could to press our case and to urge the leader of the Liberal Party, Sir Herbert Samuel, to do the same. He created a better impression than some of the Labour MPs, but Clem Attlee, the leader of the Labour Party, came up trumps. He led the fight in the House for a deputation to be received by the Prime Minister, Ramsay MacDonald, and the Cabinet.

The press covered it to a degree, but the reporters were dominated by the press bosses – who weren't overenthusiastic about our cause – so, whatever their personal sympathies may have been, our march still didn't get the coverage we felt it justified.

I suppose the earliest I became aware of the Spanish war was through some Spanish workers I knew in Liverpool. From quite early on we followed developments over there with intense interest.

In Britain at the time the dominant parties were the Conservatives and the Labour Party – which was not as progressive as I'd have liked it to be. It was divided between those who favoured supporting Spain and others who didn't want to interfere. The non-interventionist element was quite strong. The non-intervention agreement was something we had to fight against – it was an appalling thing, where the democratically elected government of Spain was denied. Terrible.

There was a lot of anger on the left but it wasn't an anger that spread throughout the population because, quite frankly, the population weren't interested – they were ignorant at that time. If you were English you didn't think about the outside world – but some of us did.

I always identified with the workers' side, the people who were standing for liberation. I was working in the docks in Liverpool; there were Spanish ships that used to come in, but in the main there wasn't much communication because I couldn't speak Spanish.

Day after day at the docks I tried to draw my mates' attention to what was happening in the world. It wasn't easy, for the order of debate was sport, sex, beer and, of course, the job. But Hitler had come to power in Germany and their trade union movement was in tatters. The trade unionists, Socialists and Communists were being pushed into concentration camps along with the Jews. Early in 1934 the Austrian trade unionists had been brutally suppressed by Dollfuss. Older trade unionists on the Trades Council were apprehensive and conveyed their fears to me, but, to my workmates, Germany and Austria were far-off countries.

My family were very strongly opposed to Fascism and all its characteristics and associates, including the British element, so-called.

Around this time I joined the Territorial Army – not so much out of patriotism but because some of my mates from the docks had joined and persuaded me to follow suit. It was good fun, and I learnt to handle a rifle, then later an eighteen-pounder gun, and I became a bombardier. The comradeship among the men was splendid, the beer in the canteen was good, too, and we got free heavy boots (useful on the docks) and overalls. The officers didn't impress me much – they were young, middle-class business types – and, to my amazement, when I went along to a Mosley meeting to protest against his Fascist policies, I found some of our TA officers among the Blackshirts. Needless to say, I watched them closely after that, and warned the men about them. We mocked them behind their backs, and any standing they might have had diminished to nought.

Within the Trades Council we formed an anti-Fascist group, giving out leaflets to people going into Blackshirt meetings and protesting inside the meetings. It was not official Labour Party policy to protest in this way – the leadership felt we should 'ignore' the Blackshirts, but that didn't seem much of a policy to me. I led groups of young Labour, ILP [Independent Labour Party] and Communist members to go and speak out at Fascist meetings – and was forcibly ejected from each meeting. Burly Blackshirts (they seemed to be paid thugs to me – the officer types weren't involved) would jump on us and lash out with knuckledusters on their hands. On more than one occasion I was thrown out of the building and left almost unconscious on the street, with a bloody nose and a black eye. The police, who were standing by, took no action.

My anti-Fascist feelings hardened when a number of Jewish refugees from Germany came to Liverpool and told us of their terrifying experiences. News was coming through from the union and the International Transport Workers' Federation [ITWF] detailing the arrest, imprisonment, torture and, in some cases, execution of trade unionists in Germany. Occasionally, when I worked on a German ship, I would make contact with a friendly German who would tell me something of the situation in his country. Polish and Danish seamen expressed their fears to me, too.

World events provided plenty of provocation for sectarian Liverpool, with the news in July 1936 of the revolt against the Spanish Republican Government. A wave of sympathy for the elected Spanish Government and the Spanish people swept through the labour movement, and there were many meetings where resolutions were passed urging support for them.

Right from the very early stages I was prepared to go to Spain – and naturally I was on the side of the workers' movement, and identified with them. I organised meetings with Spanish seamen and with members of the Spanish community in Liverpool. They were worried by the situation but proud of their government, and they urged me to do all I could to drum up solidarity. Spanish aid committees were set up and the National Council of Labour called for support for the International Solidarity Fund for the relief of distress among the Spanish workers.

In August 1936 Ernest Bevin praised 'the heroic struggle being carried on by the workers of Spain to save their democratic regime'. The *Daily Mail* and other right-wing newspapers, however, took a different view and printed scathing attacks on the constitutional government. The Catholic Church, for the most part, was equally tendentious. In some churches Franco was proclaimed as the defender of Christianity against atheistic materialism, church burning, outrages against nuns and other things too horrible to relate. A few Catholic Labour city councillors swallowed the propaganda and declared their support for Franco – but they were the exceptions.

Franco and his insurgents, backed by Hitler and Mussolini, made considerable advances in the early months of the civil war, and the Spanish Government was under enormous pressure. The UK's non-intervention policy became a cruel masquerade, preventing the legitimate government from getting the supplies it needed from Britain and France. Strong feelings of frustration led to a flow of volunteers going to Spain to fight on the government's side.

I had no doubts as to where I should be, and quickly offered my services at the Aid Spain office in the Haymarket in Liverpool. I had some territorial training and was young and fit – but my hopes were soon dashed. I was told I would be of greater service to the Republic by carrying on my activities among the dockers and seamen. Because of my many contacts, they asked me to assist in recruiting specialists for the Republican navy and for the International Brigades. I did this, but always with a feeling that I should be going to Spain as well.

Recruiting was a personal thing. I was in touch with forces of the Republic and so, if there were people who were likely to be useful, I contacted them – people like Calvin Cole, who was a seaman and who had served in the navy. I mention just one name, but there were many others whom I was able to recruit to go to Spain. I was just a young man, and the only military training I'd had was with the TA – but at least I'd got that, and I'd been prepared to go from the very beginning. With the Territorials I was with the artillery, but I couldn't really recruit among them; however, I did recruit among people I knew who had military training – some had been regular soldiers who'd been in training after the First World War.

There was no training in this country for the recruits – which was why I particularly tried to recruit people who'd got some experience. We didn't want to send people out who had no experience with weapons. There were quite a lot of people who were enthusiastic to go but who had no military training – in fact most of them – but they simply wanted to go and support the Republic.

Despite being involved in campaigning as the Labour candidate in the Croxteth Ward, I continued to be involved with Spain, and news of reverses suffered by the government forces threw a black shadow across my life. We only got intermittent news of the fighting in Spain – and the press wasn't giving a very good picture. We read the *News Chronicle* – which had a reporter in Spain – and the workers' press – the *Daily Worker* – but that was about it.

A number of Liverpool lads had gone to join the International Brigades and I took a keen personal interest in their progress. Early in 1937, many British lads were killed at the Battle of Jarama, including about twelve from Liverpool – some I knew well – and I grieved for them. I had the job of going to see the families of those killed or wounded in Spain, which was pretty terrible, but, as I was the Liverpool organiser of the forces supporting the Republic, I felt responsible. I worked along with a lad named Joe Cummings who was engaged in work for Spain full-time, recruiting and helping wherever possible. There were no telegrams from Spain to inform people – so we had to tell them in person. Often it was young wives with their children. That was a very sad thing. They weren't opposed to their husbands or fathers following their conscience, but it was sad that they had to suffer the loss.

To carry the message of the death of a loved one is

distressing at any time, but when the details are unknown and the death has occurred in battle in a foreign land, it is doubly difficult. Most widows and dependants were suffering dire poverty and the help we could give was small. We tried to raise money wherever we could to support the widows and children, through the local trade union branches – but otherwise, if they were widowed, they'd just get the widows' pension from the state. It was an awful situation.

I repeated my request to be allowed to join the International Brigades, and this time was told that in principle my application was accepted, but I was still needed to work in the union and the Labour Party to gain as much support as possible for the Spanish Government. I spent a lot of my spare time organising collections and arranging meetings.

I was disappointed by the efforts of my own union and the TUC to help Spain. Financial support from that quarter was negligible, and I had the feeling that people in high places were washing their hands of the whole business. I began to wonder how our leaders would have reacted under Hitler had they been leaders in the German labour movement.

I told the union branch committee and a meeting of the members that I intended to go to Spain. Many members urged me to stay because they seemed genuinely to feel that a lot of rank-and-file influence in the union would be lost if I went. The branch chairman, a moderate man, was very upset and also urged me to stay. I stood firm and tried to explain in simple terms just what was involved. For many, I truly believe that Spain and the terrible problems facing its people became a living reality at last. My closest friends on the docks promised me they would continue to work hard in the union while I was away.

During this period I met, for the second time, Evelyn, whose husband George Brown had been killed in Spain at the Battle of Brunete in July 1937. George Brown was the well known District Organiser of the Communist Party in Manchester and had been a good friend of mine. She had been working abroad, in the underground movement against Fascism, and had taken many risks in doing so. The death of her husband was a deep personal wound, which only time could repair, yet her mood was not to grieve but to fight on. My admiration for her spirit was more than matched by my growing love for her. We both knew, without putting it into words, that if I returned from Spain we would marry.

For many men who went it wasn't a sense of adventure by any means. It was a feeling that we were on the right side – the side of justice. Essentially Franco was a Fascist, and he represented Fascism – the Fascism of Mussolini and Hitler was identified with Franco and he identified with them. For us it was the battle against Fascism, including our local Mosley crowd, and that inspired me and encouraged me to do what I could against it, even if it meant laying down my life for it. All of us who supported the Republic felt it was absolutely right to give them whatever help we could, and, since I was organising and recruiting people, I felt that I should go early on – and, what was more, I had TA training, for what it was worth.

Of course, there was a public opposition to our going. Wherever they could, sections of the press denounced us as a 'popular front'. In the main, apart from the *News Chronicle* and the left-wing press, the tendency was to support the Establishment. It was certainly not going head over heels in support of the Republic.

As for my mother and father – well, I was always very independent, and so I told them I was going, and that was it. My father was an old soldier – and I don't think he was worried about it. There was no great heart-rending emotion – we liked each other, but we weren't close. As I was very independent, I'd be away a lot – hunger marches and so on – so they were used to my ways.

I was on the National Docks Committee of the Union so I thought I'd go and see Ernest Bevin – and I told him I was going to Spain. I think he felt it was a young man's wild approach, he thought I was a bit too far to the left for his liking – he was very right wing. He wasn't unsympathetic but he wasn't overenthusiastic. However, when I left I took a letter of support from Bevin – but it was very carefully worded.

This was the first time I had really left England – I may have been to France for a day. We had been recruited as a group and knew each other before we went, and there was a good relationship among us from the beginning. About a dozen of us came by train to London, and then to Newhaven, where we got on the boat, landed in France, then made our way to Paris, where we were looked after and given food. Underground activities against Fascism had been concentrated in

Paris for some years, and it became the focal point for the mobilisation of the International Brigades. I led my group of volunteers to the headquarters there, proceeding with the greatest caution because of the laws against recruitment in foreign armies, and the non-intervention policies of both Britain and France. From London onwards, it had to be a clandestine operation until we arrived on Spanish soil.

Once we left Paris we got the train to Perpignan, where we met up with a lorry which took us over the Pyrenees. Our movement was illegal at the time, but I was not the least bit anxious on that journey – the Establishment was against it but they weren't going to go out of their way to make martyrs.

We travelled by coach from a town near the Pyrenees to a rambling old farmhouse in the foothills where, after a rough country meal in a barn, we met our guide, who led us through the mountain passes into Spain. My comrades accepted rope-soled canvas *alpargatas* for the long climb, but I kept my Territorial Army boots. I felt they would provide better protection against the rough terrain, and I certainly escaped blisters and cuts, which others suffered. It was an arduous journey through the dark night. For about nine hours or more we were climbing – walking one in front of the other – with occasional short spells for rest. It was a bit like a commando course. For many it was very difficult – they found the walk over the Pyrenees a great strain and many took ill on the way, but I had been in the TA and dealt with it better.

The Spanish working people were very friendly towards us – they wanted our backing and support – so the Spaniards we met really appreciated our efforts. We were their comrades, so to speak. They gave us bread and food, and we went on our way, moving by night.

I delivered the letters I was carrying to the new General Secretary of the UGT [Unión General de Trabajadores], Rodriguez Vega, an able but worried man. The letter from Bevin seemed to irritate him. In his conversation with me he scorned the way the British labour movement had failed the Spanish Socialists and trade unionists. 'Why have they not forced your government to support us? Why have they not done more to demonstrate solidarity with us in action?' I had no answers and I felt ashamed.

In my reply I spoke about the many rank-and-file activities in Britain and told him, 'I have come to fight.'

He raised his eyebrows: 'One young man . . . well . . .'

At the end of my visit to the General Secretary I was persuaded to join a group of UGT men – Spanish workers, including some ex-seamen – who were going into action at the front. I got permission and I was given a rifle, a revolver and ammunition for both. The rifle I knew how to use – the revolver I was not sure about and I handed it back.

The first fighting I encountered was pretty intense. It was in a defensive action in the Lérida area, towards the Aragón, and the fact that I had a military training and good clothing, equipment and boots was a real help. Sometimes we were in defensive positions and sometimes we were attacking, but we were always taking cover when we could.

The fighting was mainly in open ground; it was not exactly

hand-to-hand but close enough to be firing with rifles and handguns. This lasted a few weeks and I saw my first deaths there. We had to bury the dead quickly in shallow graves. Also, we weren't getting any food at this time, so we were very hungry – we had big problems getting food.

I was helped by two of the men I was with, who spoke English pretty well, but communication wasn't easy in an entirely Spanish force. If I had any doubts about the spirit and strength of feeling in favour of the Republic, they were soon dispelled. The soldiers were firm in their determination despite conditions of intense adversity, knowing that their women, old people and children back home were suffering bombing, strafing, shortages and near-starvation.

I remember one incident vividly. An old Spaniard shouted, *'Yo lucho para libertad!'* (I fight for liberty), as he dug in alongside me. The ground was hard and stony and, even with the aid of a trenching tool, it was only possible to dig a shallow strip. We had to use what natural cover was available. Laying his trenching tool on the ground, he picked up his rifle to fire at the opposing force. Franco's men sent back a hail of rifle and machine-gun fire. I looked at the unlikely soldier by my side and marvelled at his courage. He had a gnarled, bronze face, a heavy body, and was wearing the cap and overalls of a working man. He was afraid of nothing. It turned out he was an anarchist, but he typified for me the resolve of so many Spaniards, who hated the idea of a Fascist takeover. In his courage, he was reckless – a recklessness which did for him for he was killed by the return of fire. He was shot in the head and died quickly. Others around me dragged him away and later buried him in a rough, shallow grave. I kept on firing, and it was only luck that saved me from the same fate. I must have been as reckless as he was, because I foolishly insisted on wearing a black leather jacket – which wasn't the best camouflage. The jacket had been given me by friends at home, and I couldn't bear the thought of not having it with me.

After a time I was sent to the British Battalion and was asked by Sam Wild, the commander, and Bob Cooney, the battalion commissar, to act as a commissar with the Major Attlee Company. They pointed out the need for the men to feel that the movement was supporting them, and my links with the Labour Party and trade union movement were important in this respect. One was not expected to refuse an assignment and so I accepted and proceeded to study the duties of a *comisario de guerra*.

In my job as commissar I worked closely with Paddy O'Daire, the commander, and I quickly came to enjoy this. Quiet, nonchalant and friendly, Paddy impressed me greatly with his deep knowledge of military matters and his experience of life.

I was continually struck by the working-class background of most of the British and Irish who were fighting in Spain. They reminded me of stories from the First World War about [common soldier] 'Tommy Atkins'. We didn't talk much about politics, and yet they all knew why they were there. The basic loyalty to the Spanish Republic was self-evident, and relations with the Spaniards in the battalion were close and friendly. The use of rudimentary Spanish became second nature in communications between all of us.

Life wasn't easy, but a good spirit prevailed in the ranks. Food was short; our main meals consisted of beans, lentils and chickpeas, sometimes beans with dried fish in a stew, or beans with mule meat or old goat, stewed and topped off with rough – very rough – red wine. Some of the lads visited an old chap in a nearby village who, allegedly, made stew from mice, but nobody would admit to having tasted it. Needless to say, there were no cats or dogs around!

Before the Battle of the Ebro, I met up with young Ted Heath. He came out with a small group of students, while we were in training. He was then Chairman of the Federation of University Conservative Associations, and was to the right of the five-man delegation. I suppose he reflected a strand of Conservative thinking which had some sympathy with the Republic – a line more prominently followed by the Duchess of Atholl and even occasionally by Winston Churchill. When we stood around chatting that day, we little thought that our paths would cross in later years in Downing Street and other prestigious places, a far cry from the Ebro Front.

He was very sympathetic and I built up a friendship with him. It was amazing to me that a Conservative would come out there in favour of the Republic – as he was, genuinely. I established a link with him which I maintained afterwards – he was always very friendly, more so than some of the Labour Party. I say that now – but I wouldn't have said it at the time.

I found I identified more with Ted Heath than with Harold Wilson, for example.

During the visit I entrusted one of Ted Heath's left-wing colleagues with the 'Book of the 15th International Brigade' signed by all members of the Major Attlee Company, with a short message from Paddy O'Daire as commander and myself as *comisario*. It was an act of respect to our patron and we asked that the book should be delivered personally to him.

Before the Ebro, I'm bound to say that we thought we were fighting against the odds anyway, because the Germans and Italians were on Franco's side – so we were fighting quite strong forces, with not the strongest of resources in our case. So it was against the odds, but it was for the right cause, the Republican cause – at least that's what I felt. I identified strongly with the cause, and that it was justified, whatever the circumstances. Besides, I was a single man and wasn't afraid of the consequences, whatever they were.

Towards the latter part of July, the tide seemed to be turning for the Republic, as our forces advanced into areas on the other side of the River Ebro, with the aim ultimately of reopening land communications with the south. The generals may have planned recklessly and in desperation, but the men were not aware of the considerations which influenced decisions at the top, and we were glad to advance.

We finished our training at Marsa and then our company marched some twenty miles to the river. It was rough country-side – hilly – and it was very difficult to dig in the very hard, rocky ground. So we took cover where we could. There was a spring in our step as we marched towards the river, but it was past midnight before we came within reach of it. The men were grouped together in their sections. There could be no smoking or talking, for we were within metres of enemy territory. Shell bursts and machine-gun fire could be heard.

At dawn our battalion was on the move. The quartermaster had arrived with a lorryload of food, but we couldn't stop for breakfast. An artillery barrage was landing shells not far away – close enough to warm our ears. As we moved through the trees on the riverbank, enemy planes appeared in the sky above us, bombing and then strafing the area. The bullets crackled, but luckily there were few casualties.

All our brigade needed to cross the Ebro, which we did in small boats during the night – and we were shelled. But in the main we managed to get over. Pushing our way through the trees to the edge of the river, a remarkable spectacle presented itself. The river was like a lake at one of the holiday resorts back home – full of little rowing boats crossing and recrossing. Our lads got into the boats, about half a dozen at a time, and were quickly rowed across. On our right, the labour battalion was erecting a pontoon bridge.

Our elation at landing on what had been Fascist territory less than a day earlier was considerable. The boats were landing at scattered points along the bank, and I had the responsibility of getting the men of our company together.

We moved on towards Gandesa and Hill 481 – a crucial crossroads. We were up against crack soldiers – Moors – and Spanish soldiers. They were much better trained and equipped than we were. There were machine guns all along the ridge, which made it a very uneven fight – they had all the weaponry and we had very little.

Everywhere advances had been made, and the news from all sections of the front encouraged our men to keep moving, despite the terrific heat of the day and the incessant strafing and bombardment. Our company was quickly involved in fighting in the hills where Moorish troops were strongly established. The terrain provided natural cover for snipers and we suffered many casualties. It was exhausting work, climbing the hills under the heat of the Spanish sun, in clothes that were often no better than rags and with little to drink. Sometimes we went for a day without water, which we badly needed to moisten our burning lips and parched throats.

We were spread out in small groups in skirmishing order, and from time to time we were confronted by fanatical Moorish soldiers who thought nothing of stringing together a number of grenades, pulling the pins out quickly and hurling the lot at us. It was a special skill they exercised at no small risk to themselves. We had an understandable fear of the Moors, who had a reputation for vicious treatment of their enemies, so it was a relief when we got control of the situation and secured a large number of Moorish prisoners. They were a fierce-looking lot, but we treated them well, much to their surprise. A number were selected for questioning, but the information obtained was not especially helpful.

It was during this period that I conducted my first burial. A young man from London had been killed and a shallow grave prepared. As we gathered round the grave, on the rough hillside, there were no tears and little emotion – time was short and the ceremony was taking place under fire – but there was respect and determination shown as I spoke a few words. 'We shall remember him. Ken died for the cause of the people of Spain – *Viva la República española!*'

We tried at least to bury our dead, but, as casualties increased, this became more difficult. We grew hardened and impersonal. I recall coming across a dead comrade, and, before I thought of burial, I looked over his gear for any food he might have, and found, to my delight, a tin of corned beef. I shared this find with a good friend and we ate it together, savouring the delicacy, under heavy fire.

The battles were hotting up as we climbed the hills leading to the 'Pimple' – a high hill, heavily fortified by the Fascists, officially known as Hill 481. German and Italian planes were bombing and strafing, while our anti-aircraft opposition was almost non-existent. Here and there a horse or mule had been killed, and after a day or so in the heat they swelled up and the smell pervaded the countryside.

Day after day, we made attacks on Hill 481 to try to gain the summit, an almost impossible task without artillery and air support. The Fascists had placed concrete pillboxes and machine guns in key positions commanding every approach to the summit. In many places they had tied mines in the bushes: if you touched one you were blown to pieces. Above all, they had plentiful artillery and a considerable force in reserve, plus German and Italian planes in abundance.

The number of dead and wounded mounted rapidly and the British Battalion took a heavy battering. Among those killed was Lewis Clive, a former Oxford rowing blue and Labour Councillor for Kensington, who was the company commander. The news was a great shock to all of us. It was difficult to believe that such a fine, upstanding man was no longer alive. I could tell many harrowing stories of those days – so many good men died, believing to the end in the cause of democracy. Win or lose, the world needs sincerity – and in Spain it was demonstrated by so many in full measure, even unto death.

One day I had clambered up the hill with my comrades, taking cover where we could and firing at the enemy wherever he appeared. The bullets of the snipers whizzed over, grenades and shells were striking the ground, throwing up earth and dust and showering us with shrapnel. Suddenly my shoulder and right arm went numb. Blood gushed from my shoulder and I couldn't lift my rifle. I could do nothing but lie where I was. Near me a comrade had been killed, and I could hear the cries of others, complaining of their wounds. While I was lying there, to make things worse a spray of shrapnel hit my right arm. The stretcher-bearers were doing their best, but could hardly keep up with the number of casualties. I just had to lie there in the heat until the night came and then move in the dark. It was a tough time, I knew that. I didn't think I might die, but I didn't feel too good. However,

I was still determined to carry on whatever happened – but once I was wounded it meant I couldn't carry on.

As night fell, I made my own way, crawling to the bottom of the hill. I was taken with other wounded men down the line to an emergency field hospital at Mora del Ebro, where I was given an anti-tetanus injection. The hospital was like an abattoir – men who had been badly injured were all over the place, and there was blood all over us. We were lying as it were on a sunny field. It wasn't a hospital as you understand it – just in a tunnel on a hill – but all of us there were very badly wounded – including me – and there were only a few doctors.

I was taken by ambulance to a hospital at Mataró, near Barcelona, where the bullets and bits of shrapnel were taken out. My arm was out of action for quite some time and, although I was moved to hospitals at Barcelona and Santa Colomba, my wounds didn't heal easily. It was decided that I should go back to Britain.

That was my last part in the fighting, but I was still very anxious to help. With my wounds I couldn't very well go back into the field, so when I got back to Liverpool I kept busy recruiting and putting the case wherever I could. We established an office where we continued to recruit men.

I knew that the Spanish people were starving so, although I couldn't go back and fight, I did all I could to get some food over there: we organised a food ship to take a substantial amount of food over to Spain.

It was very difficult to get people to sign up to continue the fight – especially once they saw the wounded coming back. There weren't too many recruits then and the number we signed up was a lot less than at the beginning.

You couldn't say much about the country as a whole, but within the labour movement, the trade unions and the Labour Party there was sympathy and support, but there was a strong pacifist element at that time. Quite frankly, to many people, Spain was just another far-off country – it seems ridiculous now, but that's how it was.

I think that people within the left wing of the labour movement now have a stronger feeling of support and sympathy than then – there's a recognition that it was the right thing to do. In October 1938, when it came to an end, I had feelings of great sadness that we hadn't made the progress that we wanted to, but at least I could feel I'd done my bit – and done my best. I also had a strong feeling of repugnance towards those who had advocated non-intervention and who didn't want to know. I had more support from Ted Heath than I had from the Labour leaders.

I'd certainly do it all again. Knowing what I know now, I would do more to arouse the rank and file within the movement. This was the first working-class war, in which people got involved directly, rather than being in an organised force in trenches. In that sense it was genuine warfare. The number of casualties was enormous – and so were the casualties that followed after the war. People were starving and Franco was utterly ruthless.

Going back to Spain now is good to revive memories – we

like to think we played our part, and Spain is a progressive country today, quite different from then. At that time Hitler and Mussolini weren't the enemy of everyone in Britain, but at the time of the civil war there were Mosleyites – Fascists openly marching around in black shirts. The Second World War ended any idea of sympathy for Fascism.

Our cause was justified subsequently, so in a way we feel ours was a little part but in a progressive direction, justified later by the war against Fascism in general, in which the whole country was involved.

JACK EDWARDS

Born 3 January 1914 in Wavertree, Liverpool

I was an only child but I had lots of cousins. My father got torpedoed during the 1914–18 war, so I never knew him, but my mother married again after the war – she never had any more children as she was too old by then. I had twelve cousins who lived close to us, and a lot more who lived further out – it was quite a big family in that respect. The twelve cousins – we all lived in the one street, Walpole Street, so it was more or less one family. I could go to Auntie May's or Auntie Mag's and just go in and sit down – it was that kind of family.

I used to sell the *Daily Worker* down on Lime Street in Liverpool and also deliver when I was at school. I also used to deliver the *Sunday Worker* – nobody speaks about that now. It was tuppence and I used to deliver six of them every Sunday.

Our family were all Socialists, and, once they started the

Socialist Sunday School, we used to go to the services in the afternoon – and it was all Socialism. Nothing else but Socialism. We used to have that every Sunday, and in summer we used to go out on rambles in Raby Mere and Bowden Park. I grew up in a political household – they were all political, my mum, my aunts, my stepfather, my uncles and all, they were all political animals. They were all members of the trade unions, so I think that's how I came about it, you know. My mum, I remember her during the 'Freedom for Women' suffragette movement – she was in that around 1918. After that women got the vote at thirty.

I had a good upbringing – a Socialist upbringing – but I got expelled from school for a week because I wrote 'Down with caning in school' on the blackboard. So I was brought up a revolutionary. Nothing I could do about it.

I'd say there was anger within the movement but I don't think it was violent. It was fairly easygoing. I think most of the violence started in 1926 when the General Strike began, and feelings seemed to come to a head more violently then previously. I was twelve then and I remember it well. There was no coal because the miners were on strike. I had to go down to the gasworks to buy coke for the fire – we had a little truck with wheels and we used to pay two bob to fill it with coke. We used to go down there every couple of days, me and our Charlie, my eldest cousin, to bring the coke back. It never used to burn well in the fire, though.

You knew there was something going on – the miners' struggle – because it was discussed in the house. That's bound to set things going in your head. It was there all the time, the talk about it in the house. The aunties used to come together at the house on a Saturday or Sunday and they'd get chin-wagging. It was always there. We could come and go as we liked – there was no argument – or we could just sit there and listen to them. I was fourteen when I left school – a bit older than most, as you could leave at thirteen if you had a job to go to. I went to work with a small Jewish furniture manu-facturer. He was a member of the trade union. I worked for him for about three years, then he went bankrupt. Then I got a job in a garage and served my time as a mechanic. So I'd joined two unions already. I was contributing to the union – I used to pay thruppence a week. It was a lot of money, because you'd only get six bob a week and that was for you to live on and pay for everything. By the time you'd chipped that up at home, I used to get a bob – a shilling – back from my mother.

It was the early thirties then and you could sense that something was developing in the world because you used to get this feeling that things were happening in Germany. There were Jewish people coming over from Germany; before Hitler actually got to power they had started coming over and you could feel something brewing. Being in a political movement, the Young Communist League [YCL], you met it all the time. Something was going to happen somewhere. We used to organise meetings at Smith Street in the north of Liverpool, and Picton Hall – big meetings – and at the Philharmonic, which was enormous. I remember going to the Philharmonic with my mother. We had the Labour councillors and the first bloke who got in for Edge Hill was Jack Hayes. He was a Labour man – an ex-policeman. I used to do a lot of canvassing for him, down the street: 'Vote for Jack Hayes' I'd be shouting. You don't see the kids doing it now – you haven't got the feeling – the camaraderie. But it was like that in the street.

We'd seen Fascism in this country. We used to go and organise against Oswald Mosley and his gang of Blackshirts. Mosley came to Liverpool and to Birkenhead, and we had quite a few clashes in Liverpool against him. I think that's why we got a lot of Jewish lads coming into the movement then, you know, because there was a big influx of Jewish lads against Fascism, a very big amount. I think 50 per cent of the YCL were Jewish boys and girls. We had that influx after Hitler came to power, because we had these Germans who had come earlier and they met up with the newly arrived Jewish people and explained the situation. We were fighting that all the time while Mosley was here.

If it was me I'd have bloody shot Mosley if I'd had a gun. I would: I hated the bastard. He was against the working class and that was it.

Well, I thought the government's non-intervention was a load of rubbish actually, because it wasn't going to work. It was a ploy to let the Fascists go into Spain. There was no non-intervention at all as they were still allowing stuff to come in from Germany, but they weren't allowing anything into the Republic. The only thing that got through to the Republic was Potato Jones from South Wales. Captain Potato

Jones, they called him. He used to go into Bilbao with spuds. He was the captain of a coaster from Wales.

What we knew about Franco was that he was trying to take over Spain. He was a Spanish army bloke who had been in command in Morocco and he was bringing the Moors over and they were going to have a go at trying to destroy the elected government. That was the argument, see. He was a dictator and he was being backed by Hitler, and that was the reason why we opposed him. Basically it wasn't the democratic thing he was doing; it was a democratically elected government which he opposed and that's why we fought against him.

When I thought about going to Spain, I knew I was leaving with friends – it was a bit like the First World War – it was the same as the Pals.

There was one chap called Jackson who came with us when we went to Spain. He was a devout Roman Catholic. I don't know why he went to Spain really, because once we got there he couldn't understand what the Church was doing – because it wasn't doing anything. He never did find the answer as he was killed at Jarama.

My mum didn't have anything to say about me going, because she didn't know I'd gone until I got there. Ivy didn't even know I'd gone. She and I were going out together, but I didn't get engaged to her until I came home from Spain. I sent her a card from London, of the BP Building – it was a landmark at the time. I sent her a card saying 'I'm going to Spain and I'll see you when I get back'. That was it. She was in

Hope Hospital then doing her training, because her idea was, once she got her State Registered Nurse qualification, she'd come to Spain – that was her idea. We'd talked it over between us.

Before we went to Spain we were doing the collections, for food and stuff like that, and having meetings against the Fascist takeover of Spain, but there wasn't very much time for that, really, as I went in October 1936.

We were told that people might come and talk to us to stop us going, but we weren't to bother with them. There were three of us, and we went on the Imperial Bus from St John's Lane in Liverpool to London. It wasn't my first time to London – I'd been on the hunger march to London in 1933. It came from Scotland and from all over England. The great trade unionist Walter Hannington led it. Somebody met us in London and we stayed there a day or so, then we got given a ticket for a weekend in Paris. You didn't need a passport; you could buy a ticket in London for a weekend in Paris, you went Friday night, you came back Sunday. That included the train to the ferry and the boat across the Channel and then you got the train to Paris. We were met in Paris by Party members and they took our return ticket off us.

We stayed a couple of days in Paris, then we got the train down to Perpignan. From there we went to the fort in Figueres, where we did a bit of marching up and down. There were all kinds there. They were coming from all over the place. There were Germans coming from France, escaping from being under Hitler, and a lot of Italians were coming through, too.

I'd never been abroad before I went to Spain. I'd been to New Brighton! Our first impressions – well, we had a load of bloody beans. And we had to wear the *alpargatas* – they were Spanish rope-soled sandals – that's all we had. Never had boots.

It seemed very backward on the agricultural side of it, because in places men and women were pulling a plough and when they were doing the wheat they were throwing it up in the air, letting the husks blow away. Prior to that they had the donkey going round crushing it, and then they were throwing it in the air. It was very backward. Where I lived outside Liverpool it was an agricultural area, but we had tractors for wheat to cut it and put it in bags. It wasn't so there – very, very backward. All the villages had a well: they didn't have taps in their houses. You all went to the well to get your water. And they had the big jars in the house that they used to keep the water. When I spoke to them they had no idea about the outside world. They seemed to be encapsulated in the past. Even when you went into cities like Madrid and Valencia, they had trams and things like that, and cars, but when you went out into the agricultural areas outside the towns, it was very backward. And a lot of them couldn't read or write, the Spanish lads. No one went to school. It seemed unusual to meet somebody who hadn't been to school, who couldn't read or write. When we were fighting with Spanish boys they couldn't write letters home, to tell their parents how they were, and that struck me as very, very odd. I mean, everybody in England could write a letter and get a stamp and put it on, but they didn't know the basics.

When we were with the Spanish people, we mainly had rice or beans or a bit of chicken or pork, and another thing, *baccalau*, salt fish. They used to do that. We once had fresh fish when we went to a village just outside Valencia. They went out and caught fish. Otherwise there wasn't a lot of food, really. They had *garbanzos* – chickpeas – beans, rice, always had plenty of greens and oranges, plenty of oranges, but no apples.

I had no money to take with me – we never had none. Bloody hell; if you had half a dollar you'd have been a millionaire. But we got plenty of cigarettes – the Gauloises and Spanish and American cigarettes.

I imagine there were about three to four thousand people at Figueres. We were only there a few days then we got the train to Barcelona. We didn't do any drill – only marching up and down – and we didn't have any bloody guns! The first gun we got our hands on was an old-fashioned machine gun. I got that in Madrid and it was a Colt machine gun from Russia with 1905 stamped on it. You had to fill the belts first, and then fire it – but it had a pistol grip, not like the modern ones we got later.

We knew what it was about; we knew there was one thing to do: we were going to beat Fascism, that was the main aim. We had a lot of political talk and when we came from Madrid to Madrigueras we had a political commissar. At Madrigueras we got training for about a month or so, with this bloody machine gun. Later on we got rifles from Mexico. We had British officers – some of them had been soldiers before. There was one, Joe Hardy from Sheffield, who'd been in the British army. I think he'd been in fourteen years. He'd been in India and was quite a knowledgeable chap about war. I think he got made a sergeant.

We British were in Madrigueras, the French were in another village, the Americans in another, all round Albacete before we went to Jarama. When we went we all went together. We had no brigade title – we were just part of the Spanish army. We English were sent back to Madrigueras for training, and then we became the 16th Battalion of the 15th Brigade. The French and Germans, they each had their own battalion numbers. Then they split us up and gave us names – the André Marty, the Harry Pollitt and the Dimitrov Battalions. The Scots people called themselves Willie Gallagher's Battalion – there were a lot of Scots.

I imagine there were some three to four hundred in our battalion. It was quite a big battalion, actually, what with all the Scots and Welsh. It was only later on that they tended to separate them into Scots and Welsh. We had our own cooks. With the English battalion we had English cooks. But there was no qualified cook. They didn't have stoves, so we used to light a fire and put the pots on the top. It wasn't an army. It didn't do the stuff an army did. I mean, in 1914–18 they did have these portable kitchens they could use, but we never had anything like that.

Our Spanish colleagues were very good and they looked after me. If there was anything I needed, they would make sure I had it – and I found them all very sympathetic wherever you went in Spain. You didn't have to buy anything and wherever you were you could always get a cup of coffee.

The people understood what we were fighting for. There were no Basques fighting with us but we had a lot of Murcians and they were very, very poorly educated. They were agricultural workers but they had been trained by the Republican army – they were very well disciplined.

At our first action, the siege of Madrid, we arrived and straight away they put us on the front line in University City. We were there about three or four weeks, but I didn't see much action – it was more house-to-house fighting. We knew that if the Fascists had broken through there they would have cut the road to Valencia. We weren't frightened. In Madrid it was like trying to get to grips with something you couldn't get your hands on. But I wasn't frightened of anything. I would have gone anywhere, done anything. We couldn't see the enemy – that was the trouble.

I met Ernest Hemingway in Madrid. I was only with him for an hour or so – we were having a drink in Puerta del Sol. I didn't know who he was; I only learnt after the war.

In the next action at Jarama the enemy were firing from a distance – then they just came over the top and we were fighting at close quarters. We desperately needed bayonets but didn't have any – but the enemy had bayonets. There was one on our rifle but we didn't all have a rifle each. We had this old machine gun which wasn't a lot of good at close quarters! They retreated again then, I think it was on the third day, we were going to go over the top once more, and I got wounded in the right foot. I was taken off pretty quick. I remember getting taken to Chinchón and I think it was the next day they put us on a train and took us to Castellón de la Plana. At the hospital, I met Herbie Booth, who was very badly injured – his leg was shattered. And Joe Hardy – his leg was bad, too – and another lad from London, a dark lad. I didn't realise until afterwards how many people we'd lost. No idea, really, because once you arrived there were only Spanish newspapers to read. You didn't get any English newspapers. And the Spanish newspapers never published figures of people wounded – nothing like that was published in the newspapers. You used to see reports of battles and they made it appear that nothing had happened. We had no English books while we were in hospital. I was in that hospital a few weeks and while I was there I met a nurse called Faustina, and she used to take me out in a wheelchair down to the port. Faustina only spoke Spanish – but we got by. You'd be surprised how you'd get by. But while I was recovering I really wanted to get back in there. This was early 1937.

When I was feeling better they sent me up into the mountains for a rest in a big hotel. Then Benesal for about a month: then, when we were fit, they took us to Benicasim. From there I was sent to Albacete, to the autopark – because I was a motor mechanic.

The unit I was sent to for training was an American outfit,

where I met up with Canadians, Australians and Cubans – and it was a transport outfit. They had French Fords, and big Russian trucks. They had two men to each truck and I was with Maurice Drorlais – a French Canadian. I was a qualified driver so I had an HGV licence, and we'd be sent to different outfits to service them – taking provisions and staying with them to see if they wanted anything. Then we'd return to the autopark when they no longer needed us. We kept all the units supplied and we were with them through the fighting at Teruel, then we went to the Aragón with them.

We still had discussions among ourselves – and they were hot-headed some of them – but they came down to common sense most times. You could always have a good discussion with the Americans or Canadians. The war didn't actually take over the discussion, though it had a big part to play in it. There were always discussions about what was going on at home, in America and in England. We were very active mentally. We had all kinds in the outfits. There were two Cuban black people, and the Americans had black people – there were quite a few from America and New York taxi drivers. It was great talking to them, though they had the American twang and dialect. There was Jack Freeman, Solly Newman, Dave Thompson and Jim Berét. The bloke in charge was called Clark, a Texan, who spoke Spanish, and was just called Tex.

Our vehicle never got attacked. There weren't that many planes really, you know. I mean, when you come to think of it now there were very few aircraft. We had some Russian ones but there weren't that many of them. Even in the last war in England, the number of aircraft we had in the air was surprising. There wasn't anything like that, nowhere near like that.

We saw more fighting around Teruel and Aragón. At Teruel we were stationed just outside the town itself, in a village, and I know it was bloody cold because we had some oranges and they got bloody frozen. That's how bloody cold it was. Then we were just taking munitions up to the Spanish outfits, to their rifle brigades. Then we went to Aragón, taking stuff over there; we were supplying them with munitions and food. We had to go to the *Intendencia* – the food quarters – and a Spanish bloke always came with us as he had the requisition note for the food for the outfits which used to cook it on the spot there. We were seeing a lot of the war – the rear part of it and the front. You got an idea what was going on in different places because you met other drivers. When you went to a Spanish outfit they only spoke Spanish. You didn't get to know anything, really. I had two years' fighting and it was always with Spanish people. They were all for it, you know – they weren't despondent in any way. They always thought they would win the war; they always thought that.

My worst moment was when we were coming out of Aragón and we had to divert to get out. We just hung up on the bloody roadway there. That was the worst. Another thing that worried me was in Teruel, when I saw the amazing sight of the aurora borealis – the colours going up and down in the sky – red and green. It was night and the sky was lit up, and it was only when I read about it in the paper that I found out what it was. That was a bit of a shock.

We felt really downhearted about Guernica after the aerial bombing by the German air force. We were in a bubble – there were just rumours. That's all you got, rumours.

By the middle of '37, well, we thought we were doing all right, to tell you the truth – but, then, I had never envisaged losing. We weren't going to lose: we were going to win, irrespective of what happened. I did think, though, when we were coming out of Aragón, that it was getting a bit tough, because we were retreating all the while. We weren't advancing, we weren't making any progress. It seemed then that we were going to lose, but we never gave up hope, even at that point.

I only found out how things were later on, when a sergeant took me to see the colonel and he told me the League of Nations had said all the foreigners would have to leave. Well, I couldn't see any bloody sense in it – how I was going to get home? He said I was going to go to Valencia. Well, that was on the other side of Spain and not on the side where I could get back home. But we were under the impression it was all the Germans and the Italians who were fighting with us who'd be getting out, but that was not the case. It was only the International Brigades that were ordered out. I think that is why the Republicans lost the war to a certain extent. Once the League of Nations had said all foreigners must go, that's when they started coming out of the Ebro. That was in late '38.

I went down to Valencia and in the barracks there were

French, Germans and Italians – there were two or three hundred of us – all waiting to go. One night they told us we were going down to the port and we boarded a ship. I was bloody glad to get out. We left Valencia one night in a boat round to Barcelona. Then we walked from Barcelona into France.

The Germans I met had come from France. They had left Germany and gone to France and then they came to Spain. I often wonder what happened to them when they went back to France again and the Second World War broke out. And, of course, what happened to the Italians who had come to fight Fascism?

Looking back, it was a simple choice, really. It was either fight or we were going to end up with bloody Fascism. You've got to realise, I was politically motivated, I was in a political organisation and we knew what was happening and we thought that, if we didn't stop it then, we would never stop it – and that's why I volunteered and went to Spain. That was the reason behind it, no other reason; it was against Fascism.

The rest of the boys had come back in '38, but I came back February '39 on the train on my own. My mum was there and my stepdad, my auntie and two or three cousins. Ivy was still in Manchester. They didn't know I was coming home until I sent a telegram from London to tell my mother what train I'd be on. It was wonderful to see them. It had been two long years. When I got home I sent a letter to Ivy and told her, and that I would see her on Saturday. We couldn't phone from Spain – there weren't any. The villages didn't have telephones.

Not many people had telephones in Liverpool either. And letters from home – every now and then you'd get one, but it would be bloody old when you got it. Any post would come first to the regiment and they'd send it on to us wherever we were. It all took time. When you got a letter you'd read it three or four times.

I feel it was very sad to lose so many people – so many fine people – but then it was for a good cause. I think they went knowing that, really, that this could happen. But you don't expect it to happen to you. I still think they should be remembered for what they'd done, for fighting in the civil war, and that's why I like to see all these little plaques in the towns and villages in Spain. It is the same in France; you'll see plaques where the Resistance people were shot – fighting and refusing to give in to Fascism.

People think of it as a forgotten war, but it should be remembered, really, as a fight against Facism, for democracy; that's the main part of the war. It's becoming a forgotten war because it wasn't worldwide. It's only because people keep bringing it up now and again, but I'm surprised it's not taught in the schools – they should teach it out of respect for democracy. That would leave behind the legacy of the Brigaders – something that people could remember us for.

Yes, I'd do it all again. I think if you've got firm beliefs and you've been brought up with them, you would do it again. I wouldn't hesitate. I'm a bit bloody old now, but there you go. I don't think the young people of today would go – they're not politically aware or active – there's no politics going on at the moment. We had the hunger marches because people were very, very short of food. There was big unemployment and it was all politically linked. I don't think you get any discussion about politics now in schools. I don't think you get politics discussed at all. I don't think my grandchildren talk about it – they've all got good jobs and that's it – the end of life. But to me that wasn't the end of life.

I'd say my dream never died. I came home in the February '39 and within a year I decided that I was going to join up again, this time in the RAF. I joined because it's the same bloody fight. There was a big argument politically: whether the fight against Hitler was the same fight as we had in Spain – and I argued it was. A lot in the Communist Party said we should be antiwar, but I never agreed with that. I said it's the same bloody war, actually, that was going on when Hitler started in September; it was the same war as was going on in Spain and I volunteered for the RAF and came out in 1946. The day my daughter was born!

BOB DOYLE

Born 12 February 1916 in Dublin
Died 22 January 2009 in London

I was one of a family of five – two brothers and two sisters. I was the second youngest to my sister Eileen. It was the time of the 'Troubles' and we were living in the North King Street area.

Soon after the youngest child, Eileen, was born, my mother, whose father was from a mixed marriage – Protestant father and Catholic mother – was found to be incapable of looking after her children and confined as a religious lunatic to Dublin's Grangegorman asylum. My father, Peter Doyle, was a fireman – he shovelled coal into hoppers on ships. While he was away at sea, my eldest sister, Josie, who was about nine, looked after us and tried to run the home when my mother was in the asylum. She was the only one who had a bit of sense.

Soon we came under the attention of nuns in nearby Eccles

Street, whom I thought to be the Sisters of Charity. My aunt came one day and brought us up to the convent. They took us into their care, and that was the last we were to see of any relative for nine years.

At the age of five, me and my sister Eileen, aged two, were placed with the Byrne family; my brothers Christie and Peter were sent to some place in Cork. Only Josie stayed at home.

During the mushroom season, I would get up at six to beat the other kids and run round the fields in my bare feet for the mushrooms, pissing on my feet to keep them warm in the early morning dew. A local farmer would pay me fourpence a day to frighten the crows off the wheat. With a cocoa tin pierced at the bottom, you'd put a bit of carbide, used for bicycle lamps at the time, spit on top of it, and, with the lid pressed on, put a lighted match at the bottom – then stand clear for the bang. It certainly frightened the crows!

I was twelve when, out of the blue, Mother Superior told me that myself and Eileen were going to Dublin to my parents. My mother was now back home. We were in 30 Stafford Street, now Wolfe Tone Street. My parents, brothers and sister were strangers whom I could not recollect ever having seen before.

Life was miserable at home for us, the two youngest. My mother would make us go to regular early Mass, which we hated, and, while we could only afford condensed milk and meat bits from Moore Street, she would give money to the priests at Dominick Street chapel for Masses to be said 'for the repose of the poor souls in purgatory'. At one stage the priest told her that her duty was to her children, and she should keep the money and feed them. Everything pawnable went into Brereton's pawn office in Capel Street on Mondays, even a new pair of sheets.

My mother would give me a penny to go over to the Whitefriar Street chapel to light a candle and pray to a certain saint to get me a job. (The Carmelites there have the shrine to the apostle St Jude, popularly known as the 'patron saint of hopeless causes', and opposite, in the same side chapel, the shrine with relics of St Valentine.) It gradually dawned on me that neither God nor the saints would perform this miracle, but I thought perhaps my prayers were answered when I saw the following advert in the *Dublin Evening Mail*: 'Young boy wanted to train as butler'.

I replied to the advert and was taken on by a family named Patterson in Sandymount, Dublin. Here I got a good bed and food and five shillings a week. I found myself being a 'houseboy', doing all the cleaning, polishing the shoes and emptying the chamber pots. On receiving the guests for the weekly bridge party, I was instructed when opening the front door to remain unseen by walking behind the door.

It was 1931–2 – the time of the General Election when [Eamon] de Valera was making his bid for power under the slogan 'Get your husbands off to work', which I took to mean that he would create more jobs. Mrs Patterson hated my support for Fianna Fáil. She thought de Valera was a Communist – the devil in hell. After three months of subservience,

I'd had enough. I was a good worker, but I was made to feel like a slave.

I told Mrs Patterson I was leaving and asked her for a reference. She furiously took a piece of paper and wrote 'honest'. I tore it up, slung it on her table and returned to Stafford Street – I knew that her curt reference would be no good to me as proof of experience and character for the next job. In those days you couldn't get a job without a good reference.

Despite the misery, poverty and religious hysteria, Dublin that summer was great – a unique and beautiful city surrounded by sea and mountains. It was delightful to see the thousands setting out on the weekends towards Blackrock and Dollymount. These were the two huge beaches on either side of Dublin Bay, easily reached by any Dublin family with a pram on a sunny day.

One day my brother and I decided to nick the B&I [British & Irish Steam Packet Company] mooring boat and row to Liverpool. It was a heavy carvelled rowing boat, used by two stevedores to take the lines out for mooring the passenger and freight boats from Liverpool. We nicked it in the early evening and set out for where everyone seemed to be emigrating.

We got as far as Ringsend at the mouth of Dublin Bay when the tide turned and heavy winds set in. My brother, with more sense than me, decided to abandon ship and pulled in against the sea wall. He climbed out while I was calling him a cowardly so-and-so. I too had to abandon ship. We walked back – I doubt if we tied up the boat. I would have to wait for another opportunity to get to Liverpool – the land of hope.

By now I had started to take part in the demonstrations by the unemployed for work or full maintenance, and to fight against the rising tide of Fascism. By this time Italy had been completely taken over, and there were a number of countries that had dictatorships or had gone Fascist – like Portugal, Hungary, Poland and Bulgaria – and, from 1933, Germany.

When the Blueshirts – the Irish Fascists – caught me on a demonstration through D'Olier Street I was surrounded by a crowd of them. They got me down a laneway off Dame Street and were hammering me. The police came and they joined in and then arrested me, dragging me up to O'Connell Bridge to an inspector who was sympathetic.

When I was alone with the inspector for a moment, he said, 'Can you run?'

I said, 'Yes', and was across the bridge like a hare.

There was a lot of violence between us and the Blueshirts. On another occasion we were waiting for a Blueshirt march – we tried to stop them and I got a knuckleduster in the eye and ended up in the Mater Hospital.

I had by now acquired a little knowledge of upholstery, working as an apprentice for a little man who was an upholsterer in a basement in a slum in Dominick Street for two and six a week, and I earned a few bob repairing chairs for the rich in Merrion Square. It was 1934 and I had saved enough to make another attempt to get to Liverpool – this time on the B&I cattleboat, which cost about ten shillings at the time.

I felt sad as we sailed down the Liffey, singing to myself 'Come back to Erin, Mavourneen'.

In Liverpool I stayed at the Salvation Army in Park Lane at one and six a night. I saved what money I could by filling my pockets from the mountains of Brazil nuts on the docks, bound for Libby's, and at night patronising the different Gospel halls which enticed you to come in and pray with tea and sandwiches.

I tried for a job on the Mersey Tunnel, which was then being built, but had no luck, so when my money ran out I tried the Sailors' Home for a bed and ended up sleeping around the landing stage until I was sent to Father Berry's Catholic Home. Here, after a while, I was given a ticket and sent back home. The whole episode lasted about two or three weeks, and I came back again to the North Wall of the Liffey on the cattleboat, feeling disappointed.

I didn't last long at home this time. I remember my father chasing me around the two rooms we had – he was wild to get hold of me. I think it was the drink. I managed to escape out the door and got cheap digs round the corner in a two-room flat where I shared a room with Kit Conway – who was later to die in the Spanish Civil War. He was a well-known IRA activist and a legend in his native Tipperary during the fighting against the Black and Tans and the Pro-Treaty crowd. For his troubles he got a bullet through his mouth and ended with a very slight lisp.

Kit was my inspiration – a military instructor and a strict disciplinarian. He had earlier recruited me into the first

Dublin Battalion of the IRA. We used to train in the fields west of Cabra doing drill and extended formations, which was to prove useful later in Spain. On weeknights we practised dry-firing with revolver and rifle in the basement of 41 Parnell Square. I was placed in the Engineers, going out to the Dublin Mountains with dynamite and plenty of ammunition for rifle practice.

Kit used to keep a tommy gun under the bed, with a case of ammunition. He was an expert – he could take it apart and reassemble it with his eyes closed. He seemed to do a lot of nocturnal work, sometimes bringing back a revolver. Being a prominent Republican, he was often followed by a Special Branch man. He told me he could sometimes manage to slip around the detective, get him from behind and take his gun off him. He'd come straight back to the flat and pass me the revolver, and give me the price of the cinema around the corner, until the heat died down.

From the beginning of 1936 I was hearing more about Spain. It was everyday news. I read all the propaganda I could get my hands on in Dublin. There was a committee formed of those who went to Spain, and we got all the information from them – we knew as much about Spain as we would have if we'd been there – and we all wanted to stop the Fascists. The propaganda of the Catholic Church and the official press was 100 per cent in support of Franco's military revolt. It was a tremendous campaign, preaching at Mass and the missions about the need to support Franco, a gallant Christian gentleman, defending the Catholic Church in Spain.

Within such left-wing circles as the Republican Congress, it was, despite the propaganda, not so much a question of going to fight in Spain as of giving every aid to Republican Spain. Our response sprang out of the recognition of the danger of Fascism. We were very conscious that the Nazis had come to power in Germany in 1933, and that General O'Duffy was intending to follow in their footsteps. Although the Irish hierarchy was strongly behind Franco, it seemed to me that the bishops never condemned the Blueshirt movement. Did the Church support the Blueshirts? Well, tacit support – that was the right word.

I thought there was a danger that Ireland would go Fascist, and that was one of the motivating factors in making up my mind to go to Spain. I didn't know much about Spain – but I certainly knew that my thoughts were that every bullet I fired would be against the Dublin landlords and capitalists. Furthermore, I always had the habit of believing that, whatever the Church said politically, the opposite was true. That was one of the reasons why I was on the side of the Spanish Republic right from the start.

I was twenty in 1936 when the Spanish war broke out on 18 July, with the revolt of the generals against the democratically elected government of the Second Republic. Franco declared that, if necessary, he would shoot half of Spain. All were subject to the most extreme punishments by military tribunal for the possession of arms, for participating in political meetings or conferences, for the use of print or the possession of documents or papers destined for publicity,

ou Kenton, born to a Jewish-Ukranian family, served as an ambulance driver for ʋo years.

fter all these sacrifices, did we achieve anything? I think we did! I am proud of having gone d I would do it all again."

Nurse **Penny Feiwel** tended the wounded under horrendous conditions on the front line.

"War is a terrible thing – I think it's the worst thing that can happen. Such a lot of needless slaughter and misery."

After being hit in the shoulder and seriously wounded at the Ebro in 1938, **Jack Jones** spent the rest of the war recruiting soldiers for Spain. He later became the General Secretary of the Transport and General Workers' Union.

"For many men who went it wasn't a sense of adventure by any means. It was a feeling that we were on the right side – the side of justice."

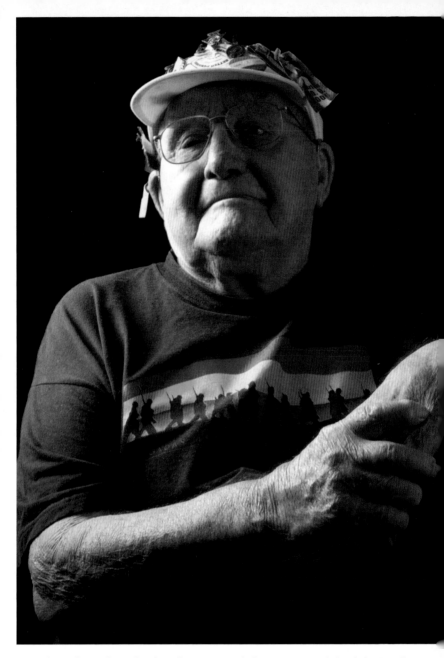

A mechanic by trade, **Jack Edwards** was wounded at Jarama. He joined the RAF in the Second World War.

"We knew what it was about; we knew there was one thing to do: we were going to beat Fascism, that was the main aim."

ob Doyle joined the IRA as a teenager and spent eleven months in a Fascist oncentration camp. He was released in 1939.

he worst moments were the beatings. Everyone was beaten. We kept going because we were nvinced about the cause…"

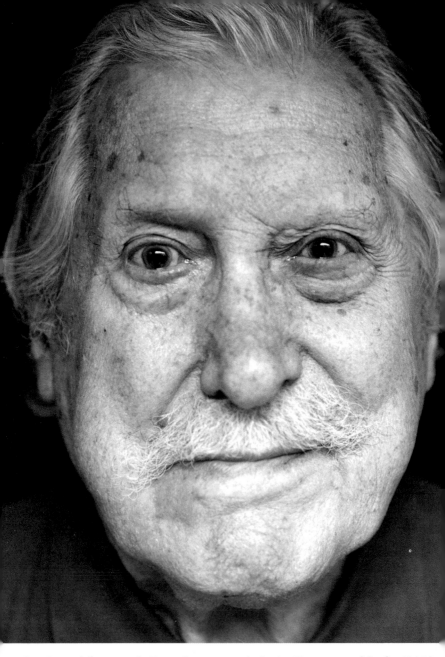

Sam Lesser left a career in Egyptology to serve in Spain. He was one of the first British volunteers. After fighting in Madrid he was one of only six left out of a unit of thirty-six.

"The gutter was literally flowing with blood, and the smell of the blood of these poor people mixed with the smell of the lime trees."

After being on the front line **Les Gibson** became seriously ill with colitis but went back to fight after his recovery.

"When they came out and were walking across this open ground, I let fly with it. The first one nearest to me went down and never moved – never moved. I know I got one back for one of our boys."

Paddy Cochrane served as an ambulance driver on the front east of Madrid. Wounded by a hand grenade, he spent the night in a ruined house before being rescued by an American soldier.

"I always felt it was worthwhile. I always felt very serious about it and there were so many people who were of the same mind as myself."

for those who left their place of work in breach of contract, and for insults or any acts of aggression against the armed forces.

It was monstrous that those in revolt were now declaring as rebels all those who had participated and won in the democratic elections. To this barbarism was added the full support of the Catholic Church. The Cardinal Archbishop of Toledo declared that the war between Spaniards was a holy crusade, and that Spain could not be pacified without the use of arms. The Bishop of Cartagena, Monsignor Díaz Gomara, thundered, 'Blessed be the cannons if the Gospel flowers in the breaches they blow open.' Franco even claimed that the Pope would grant one hundred indulgences for every red killed.

In Málaga, which was conquered by Italian and Franco troops in February 1937, more than five thousand were executed without trial for being sympathetic to the Popular Front [the coalition of left-wing parties]. Men and women, peasants and intellectuals, were shot on the beaches and against the cemetery walls by Italian mercenaries.

I learnt that the last group going out from Ireland to Spain had already gone, and that there was no group being prepared that I could join, so I decided I'd get there under my own steam. I set out on the B&I boat to Liverpool and from there to London, where I stayed at the Salvation Army in Great Peter Street in Westminster. I knew nobody, so, after a few weeks trying calling into jobs, I got one as a kitchen porter – like Ho Chi Minh – at Lyons Corner House in Piccadilly

Circus for a couple of months, bringing down the milk and cream for twenty-four shillings a week. Luckily for me they had a bed for resting when you'd an hour or two off work.

When I'd saved enough money, I got my brother Peter to come with me and together we left for Jersey in the Channel Islands. It was a step towards Spain for me, and in Jersey I lived cheap in digs for two months or so. I first worked mixing fertiliser, and then I was working on the spuds, and tying up tomatoes. I saved enough for the next stage to St-Malo on the ferry, where I got the train straight to Marseilles. Peter stayed on in Jersey.

In Marseilles I could only afford to stay at the Salvation Army for two nights, so for a month I slept on park benches and under railway trucks on the siding in the daytime, it was so hot. I spoke no French at all – it was real hoboing. I was bumming my food from British ships to conserve what little money I had. The sailors were good with what they didn't need for themselves.

I waited and watched – every day I would go around the docks looking for information of ships plying the Spanish route. Eventually, I heard of one likely to sail to Valencia. It was about 2,000 tons and was sailing under the Greek flag. I managed to get aboard and hid myself in a small anchor room. Four hours out at sea, one of the crew opened the trapdoor to inspect the anchor chain, and I was discovered – perhaps luckily, because, had they dropped the anchor, the whirling chain would have made mincemeat of me. The ship had a German or Italian non-intervention officer aboard to see that it wasn't carrying arms or volunteers to the Republic. He asked me where I was going, and what my intentions were. I told him I was going to join the International Brigades. He told me I would be arrested on arrival and deported back, to be dealt with by the British authorities. There was nowhere to lock me up, so I was free to mix with the rest of the crew – who were mainly sympathetic.

We arrived at Valencia on 8 July 1937. As the ship berthed, I made a jump for the jetty and landed on a quay below. The captain and the non-intervention officer were shouting '*Policía!*' but I ran up the jetty towards the main gate, out of the docks and into the street – where I was caught. I had no identity documents or passport on me. I was taken to Valencia police barracks for questioning, where it seemed the inspector, an anarchist, suspected I was German because of my fair hair. But he handed me over to the British Consulate and left. The Consul asked me the standard questions about where I was going and what my intentions were. I told him I had come to join the International Brigades, to which he replied, 'There is no such thing. They are hiding around Spain like rats.' I knew it was a pack of lies. He then told me that I would have to work my passage back to Britain and that I was liable to be arrested on arrival.

I had no knowledge of Spanish at the time, so I was unable to make my own investigations regarding any representative of the Republic, or the International Brigades. I had enough money to stay in a cheap boarding house and was visited by the police two nights running.

I hung around the docks all the time and discovered that a young Spaniard had deserted his ship – the SS *Calderon* – on a Spanish–English shipping line, plying between France, Spain and Portugal. I went aboard and applied for the job and was signed as a deck boy.

On 10 July 1937, after loading our cargo of fruit and wine, we set sail for Liverpool, where I reported what had happened to the secretary of the Communist Party, Frank Bright, and told him of my intentions to continue on the ship going back to Spain. My membership of the Party in Dublin had lapsed, so I rejoined in Liverpool to ensure that, while sailing to and from Spain, I could do useful work, liaising with members of the International Brigade and bringing back propaganda to Britain. We set sail for Franco's Spain with a load of steel plate, and our first port of call was Cádiz where I saw German and Italian battleships.

Wounded Italian and German soldiers were being taken aboard to be shipped back to their respective countries. I was delighted – I put them down as casualties from the Battle of Jarama, which went on for nearly a month. That was the battle where Kit Conway had fought and died – but I didn't know he was dead then. I just thought, 'They're giving them hell.'

We sailed back to Liverpool and London, and we did several trips like this, alternating between Franco and Government ports, and by now I was gaining more experience of Spain and acquiring a smattering of the language. I was now liaising with the Spanish Aid Committee in Liverpool, smuggling leaflets and posters in and out of Spain and letters to and from International Brigaders when we called at Republican ports.

Our skipper, Captain Williams, began to realise what I was up to. When he saw a Government car come down to the ship and put a load of posters through the porthole for me to bring back, just before we set sail for England, he threatened that I would be blacklisted in the shipping industry. So I decided to jump ship on the next trip to Alicante, and join my comrades at the front – but first I decided to approach the Communist Party in London to enlist for the International Brigade.

I told them that if they didn't let me into Spain to fight I would jump ship at Alicante on the next trip. They suggested that it would be better if I went their way, as I now had knowledge of Spain and the language. Within a few days a group of sixteen of us was assembled and given a weekend ticket, plus £5 expenses to get to Paris. The group was jubilant on the ferry across to Dunkirk. They began drinking and singing revolutionary songs – it wasn't difficult to guess who they were and where they were going, so I told them to shut up. They didn't listen, so I tried to distance myself, and isolated myself from them. On arrival in Dunkirk, two British detectives were waiting. They pulled them aside, questioned them and sent them back on the next ferry.

As I possessed a British seaman's discharge book and had by now obtained a passport, I walked up to the detectives just a few minutes before the train was to depart and asked them why I wasn't allowed to board, and if I was going to be prevented from continuing my journey. They asked me where I was going and I told them Paris. They asked how much money I had – I still had £5 at the time – and if I thought that was enough for the weekend.

They then asked if I was going any further.

I said, 'Where's that?'

They said, 'Spain.'

I said, 'What would I want to go there for? And in any case, I have papers, so I don't need to use my passport.' The seaman's discharge book was accepted as proof of identity at ports, so they let me through and I jumped on the train as it was pulling out.

On my arrival at the trade union centre in the Place du Combat in Paris, I reported that the other fifteen had been sent back to London. They weren't pleased with that news but I was given some francs and told about cafés to go to. I remained there for a few days until a group had been assembled to go across the Pyrenees.

We were taken to Figueres, where we were interviewed as regards what positions we would occupy or to whom we would be allocated. I was asked if I spoke any other language, and I told them I had learnt Irish at school. They considered that another language – 'That'll do,' they said. Then they asked if I had knowledge or experience of arms. I told them that through my membership of the IRA I had been taught ballistics and the use of a revolver, rifle, explosives and land-mines. It was enough for them to send me to the training school in Tarazona de la Mancha, the first stop for most British volunteers.

I was in a group of fifteen volunteers from Britain and Ireland, including the young writer Laurie Lee, who had entered Spain on his own on the night of 5–6 December. We left Figueres for Albacete, and we arrived four days later at the International Brigades' base.

The training school consisted of Spanish comrades and International Brigaders and most of the tuition was in Spanish, although we quickly learnt the commands. I became a platoon commander, taking thirty men and drilling them with wooden rifles. I never saw a real rifle or machine gun while I was there. I took them out digging foxholes and showing them how to defend themselves against attacking aircraft by crossfire. We trained with bayonets.

At night-time I had a privilege and was allowed to visit a family I'd made friends with, and used to have supper with them. The fire would be on the floor under the table at your feet to keep your legs warm – it got very cold at night.

One evening in Tarazona, [actor and singer] Paul Robeson gave us all an impromptu concert. We were told he was coming and we packed into the church – hundreds of us. Some of the songs I knew – ballads and Negro spirituals – and the response was terrific. He was inspirational.

We also received some training from a Russian officer in civilian clothes, who went under the name of Rossa. He called us together for tuition on 'How to Confront the Enemy'. He was an expert on close combat, and, if we didn't show enough guts, he'd grab the rifle himself, exclaiming, 'You are volunteers – you are worth ten of the Fascists. Attack them with hatred and determination!', all the while showing us this on his features. It was a lesson well learnt.

It must have been around February 1938 when news came of a draft being sent to the front on four lorries. I had received no instructions to be part of it, but I wanted to go, so I jumped up on the last lorry – and the others on it thought I was supposed to be there. Halfway to Belchite I was discovered and brought in front of three International Brigades officers. They asked me why I had disobeyed orders and told me that my duty was to stay in the training base and to train other volunteers who would be coming over from England. I told them I wanted to be a machine-gunner, and that I needed practical experience. They then suggested that I had come here to get experience at the expense of the Spanish people – which I hotly disputed. After being given a severe ticking off, I was allowed to stay and was put in charge of a Degtyarev machine gun, which I learnt to use on the way to the front.

We soon came under fire. We were walking along the road beside an olive grove when Italian Fiat fighters came low, strafing us and throwing small bombs or grenades at us. We quickly scattered into the grove and, when the planes had passed, I remember Paddy Tighe got out in the road and did an Irish jig. We marched on in the direction of Belchite – where we became involved in the second battle for the town's defence.

Near the church at Belchite my machine gun developed a

fault and stopped working. I threw it from me, throwing away the lock separately so that it could not be used. Fletcher, the commander of my machine-gun unit, got a bullet through the hand, so I took his rifle. We were about fifty yards in front of the church, and the enemy's bullets were hitting the church wall behind us and exploding – they appeared to be dumdums.

The Fascist troops and tanks were getting nearer. We were likely to be cut off and surrounded inside the town. I got myself in a firing position with this rifle, and I was firing between trees. I could only find a small stone for shelter, firing at the enemy who were on the hill in front. You could see the Fascists moving, so I kept firing – but they were firing back at me. I stood up recklessly, no longer caring about my own safety, and started firing until the rifle got too hot. I wanted to get killed – not from bravery but because I thought this was going to be the end. The bloke beside me was killed and he was lying there. A bullet hit the wall behind me – I don't know how it missed me. Even though I thought I'd be hit, it was a miracle I wasn't touched. There were several Brigaders killed in this position. Being in that battle was frightening all right.

Faced by more than one hundred tanks, the only weapons we had were rifles of different calibres, often with the wrong ammunition, twelve light machine guns and our anti-tank battery. Those brave men held out to the very end, singing 'Hold Madrid for we are coming'.

The church we were near offered us the best strategic

position – the best place to make our last stand before with-drawing. Its strong fortifications were practically immune to destruction from artillery bombardment – not that the Fascists didn't try. Their artillery pounded us relentlessly, and their tanks came within close range.

We were then ordered to retire about two miles from Belchite to a small height where we could barely dig even a shallow trench as the hill was so rocky. You could just get your body inside it. Then, planes came over – they appeared to be German Stuka dive-bombers, which flew around where we were occupying the height. The dive-bombers were screaming as they were dropping their bombs on us, and they were machine-gunning us. I dodged about, moving from one side of the trench to the other as the planes flew around us. We held this position for about two days. While I was there, I saw an ambulance being attacked by planes as it went past us towards Belchite. That stopped it. After a couple of days, the town fell to Italian and Moorish troops. Although we were surrounded, we managed to escape, but we had lost many very good comrades.

We withdrew towards Batea and Corbera, where reorganisation took place – the battalion was reduced to about 150 very weary men from 500 only a few days before. We rested for a couple of days – I got a new light machine gun – a Degtyarev, which was a type I'd used before. I was sitting down, cleaning it and tenderly laying the parts on the ground, when a Russian general in a big astrakhan coat came over and stood looking down at me. He started asking the interpreter questions and I wondered why he was observing me so closely. I felt proud, anticipating a compliment, but I was humiliated when he said, 'Do you realise the sacrifices that have been made to get that weapon here? If necessary, take your shirt off and put the parts on that to stop them getting dirty.'

But I had my new Degtyarev, and we were re-formed and re-equipped for the next battle. We had been marching all night, but before the sun came up on 30 March we got orders to march again to take up secondary positions moving up through Calaceite. The battalion was marching along a road in infantry formation – two single files, one each side of the road, with about five yards distance between each man. The idea was to reduce casualties if we came under fire.

We heard a terrific roar of engines down in the valley below us – like a motorised column getting nearer to us. A patrol of two was sent out to investigate, but never returned. Frank suggested that me and Johnny Lemon take my machine-gun unit to the bend a couple of hundred yards up the road to provide cover. I went forwards and the rest of the unit went past me and left me there. I received no further instructions, so I decided to fall in with my crew next to Frank. There was nothing else I could do.

Then, out of the bushes, came a Spanish forwards patrol. Suddenly we were surrounded at close quarters on both sides of the road by Franco's soldiers shouting, '*Manos arriba!*' Coming up the middle of the road between us, led by a tank, were motorcycles with machine guns mounted on the handlebars. I just had time to leave my gun beside Frank and go over and look at the tank before they opened fire. At first I thought it was ours because of the colour, so I stood beside the tank. An officer was standing in the turret. It was covered in dust, but I could see the Italian colour markings on it. I rushed back towards my machine gun and shouted, 'Crikey! They're Italian! I didn't know they had tanks.'

They opened fire over our heads at our companies behind us, shouting, *'Abajo!'* [Get down!] to us as they fired, effectively cutting us off from the remainder of the battalion, who were retreating in the confusion. The motorcycles passed us. There was a smell of cordite, the noise of men shouting and bullets flying overhead. Frank and the others already had their hands up, and I got mine up pretty quick.

Wally Tapsell was at the side of the road and he shouted to the Fascist officer standing up in the tank turret, 'You bloody fool! Do you want to kill your own men?' Wally thought they were our tanks – we all expected that the Lister Division were ahead of us, and hadn't realised that the front had broken. The officer in the tank turret opened fire with a revolver and shot him dead. It all happened so quickly – he wasn't carrying a weapon when he was shot.

We had walked into a classic military ambush, set by Mussolini's Black Arrow division. It was the day Rab Butler, the Tory Secretary of the Foreign Office under Lord Halifax, stated in the House of Commons, 'We have no proof of intervention in Spain by Germany or Italy.'

We were assembled and marched off with guns trained on us. We were all convinced that Frank would be shot right away, because, although he hadn't a badge of rank, his uniform distinguished him as an officer. It was standard practice by Franco's forces that officers were shot on capture. We were marched past long lines of Italian reserves and their mechanised equipment, with squadrons of Caproni bombers and Fiat fighters passing overhead. I was amazed at the might of our enemy and felt very proud that our side had managed to hold out for so long.

A load of Fascist soldiers came up with rifles, and they lined up in front of us so I thought they were a firing squad. We thought we were going to be shot – they mentioned firing, as I could understand some of their Spanish.

We were lined up against a barn while an Italian officer came along the line, picking out likely officers. Frank looked conspicuous and they asked his rank. 'Captain,' he replied – but then said that under no circumstances would he give any other information than his own personal details.

While this was going on, a lorryload of armed Civil Guard arrived and positioned themselves in the middle of the road in front of us. These were the backbone of Franco's internal security forces, known as 'the Executioners' – so-called because they operated behind Franco's lines, responsible for his 'cleansing' operations, picking out prisoners for shooting – which is how he controlled parts of Spain he had overrun. The Civil Guard was called to attention and an officer called out to us: 'Communists, Socialists, Jews and machine-gunners, step forwards.'

With dignity, we all stepped forwards – all the soldiers

of the different nationalities. If you got the bullets first you would have a clean death and there was no difference between the volunteers of the many countries among us. We were Jews, Communists and people of various political persuasions.

The soldiers had their rifles ready, then an argument broke out among them. The Civil Guard seemingly wanted to shoot us there and then, while the Italians seemed to want to wait for orders from Burgos, the central seat of Franco's government. While this was going on, another prisoner was taken out and beaten for information. They must have got in touch with Franco and he must have given the orders for them not to shoot us, because they put us in a lorry with some cows to wait.

The matter now seemed to be resolved, as we were ordered to move to another location, in a wired compound by a dried river bed, where interrogation took place. We had lived to fight another day. At one point, ordinary Italian soldiers were decent to us – they took from us various Republican documents we were carrying and quietly tore them up, saying it wouldn't go well for us if their officers were to find them.

We were herded into cowsheds and pigsties, moved again to a disused church in Alcañiz and questioned by the Italian secret police. Frank was taken out again by the police and told he was sentenced to death – again. The Italians had asked if he was a Communist, and he told them he was an Irish Republican, 'but, if I were a Communist, I'd be proud to say so'. We were given no food or water, and used the area behind the altar for all purposes.

On arrival at the military barracks in Zaragoza, we noticed as we entered the small square six of the Lister Division standing to attention under the Franco flag with heads bowed, facing each other. They were ordered to stand to attention until they collapsed, when they would be replaced by another of the same division.

The Lister Division were the cream of the Spanish working class, and the Fascists knew it. I felt humiliated and defenceless and, faced with such inhumanity, what could we do?

Our home for those couple of days overlooked a wire compound where the Lister prisoners were herded like cattle for slaughter. The next morning we were lined up for interview with the world's hostile press. Such papers as the liberal British *News Chronicle* were prohibited, as was anything remotely associated with progressive opinions. The British and American press reported our treatment in glowing terms. We were given a meal with an apple for the occasion. We were never to see one again for the rest of our imprisonment. At least we were safe – our names would be published in some of the papers. The argument had gone on about our rights to refuse to use the Fascist salute, and a compromise was reached to give the British military salute – but the threat that we would be shot for refusal to comply with the order quickly changed our minds. We gave the salute.

We were then taken by train to Burgos; from there we were marched ten kilometres to San Pedro de Cardeña, arriving late in the evening. The camp was a sinister and forbidding-looking fortress, and our recurring thoughts were whether we would ever get out of it alive and what would happen if the next world war began. We were afraid we'd just be left locked up for the duration and forgotten about. Escape was constantly on our minds.

We must have looked a decrepit, dirty, unshaven and disorganised lot, and we were herded with rifle butts, sticks and kicks into a barren, barn-like room. We were on the second floor, with the new arrivals occupying the first. Our beds were straw sacks, with a single blanket to protect us from the freezing cold at night. There was only one mattress between two, laid out on the ancient, dusty, tiled floor. We were packed like sardines in a tin.

The morning after we arrived we were given a special display of brutality. As the Spanish prisoners assembled on the patio below us for their breakfast of oily water containing a few crumbs, they were attacked with rifle butts, scattering them in all directions as they tried to form the lines the Fascists demanded.

After a week things changed, and the guards' fury was directed against the international prisoners. Reveille was sounded at 6 am, with the guards rushing into our quarters with rifles and sticks, while the prisoners dodged their blows by running behind columns and hiding in alcoves. I couldn't help admiring a young Moor, a deserter from Franco's forces, who, when cornered, would simply curl up and take blows which we would dodge.

As we went down the two flights of stairs, the guards would be waiting at the bottom door to lay into us as we came out. The return journey was the same. We tried to organise ourselves to make our passage less dangerous – one entering slightly behind the other – but the Fascists didn't like this show of discipline and the unfortunate prisoners at the rear would always get the worst beating. Warmer weather made our lives a little easier, but the daily beatings continued. Individual assaults were carried out in a ground-floor room known as the *'sala de tortura'*. We were fed beans and a couple of sardines in the evening from a huge cauldron on the outer patio where everyone would assemble in lines. We were fed a minimum, with the sergeant watching the rations.

We had to eat our food standing up in single file. One sweltering day early in July, thinking the guard couldn't see me because I was near to the ancient wall from which a rock protruded, I decided to sit down. Three others followed suit, but the chief guard caught us. I could hear him tell the camp commandant that he was taking us into the *sala de tortura*. I told the others it was OK – we were just going to get a few smacks. As they marched the other prisoners off to their quarters, we were kept behind and then taken to the *sala de tortura*. I was taken in while the others remained under guard, facing a white wall.

As I entered, I was surrounded by sergeants. 'So, you refused to fall in!' they screamed. Before I could answer, four of them closed in and began raining blows on my back, shouting, *'Rojo! Rojo!'* [Red! Red!] and in their frenzy they sometimes missed their target and hit each other instead. I was wearing

193

only a light khaki shirt. I managed not to scream, doubling up. I protected my face and head with my hands. Two had heavy sticks, another had a heavy strap and the chief guard his favourite 'bull's penis'. 'What had I done to deserve this?' I thought, as my knees began to buckle, and I clenched my teeth. The beating lasted ten minutes. Sweating and panting, the four called for a soldier to take me back to the others, where I had to stand at attention, facing the wall until everyone had been beaten. I could hear the shouts and blows as each was taken in.

It was very frightening, but we didn't break down – no one cried. We were put to stand a distance from a white-painted wall, and we had to stare at this wall, with the guard behind us – they couldn't put us in the lock-ups in the prison because there were a load of Germans in there who had escaped. As we stood in front of the wall we were expecting to be shot; in fact, we wouldn't have minded being shot – none of us was cowardly.

After facing the wall for about four hours, we were surprised to be sent back to our comrades instead of the dungeon, the usual destination after a beating. The dungeon was on the ground floor – it had no windows and the German prisoners were kept there. On seeing me, Frank Ryan said, 'Lift up your shirt,' and he ordered me to walk up and down among the prisoners to show them 'this is what Fascism is'. They were horrified by the welts and caked blood.

Mass was said on the outer patio, and we had to salute the flag and sing the Fascist anthem. With the Spaniards in front of us singing, we would pretend not to know the words. Behind us, out of sight of the sergeants, a couple of characters would pirouette away to a souped-up version of 'It's a Long Way to Tipperary'. The anthem would finish with the Fascist salute – the right arm extended upwards through seventy-five degrees, but the sergeants always suspected that some of us were giving the clenched salute instead, and anyone making the slightest deviation would be punished by sticks or worse.

As an indoctrinated Catholic from the year dot, the Fascist Mass seemed to me an insult to anyone who was devout. The priest, on a specially raised platform, opened the service with the Fascist salute and '*Viva Franco!*' When it came to the raising of the Host and the genuflection, those who didn't know the ritual were beaten down to their knees – they quickly learnt the routine.

The camp held more than 2,000 Spanish prisoners and some 750 Internationals, the Spanish being subjected to an intense political re-education programme which would allow them out to enlist in Franco's army if they did well. The Internationals were kept in isolation to prevent their ideologically contaminating the Spaniards.

We had nothing to drink – we had to go to fetch our water. And to eat there was just bread and sardines. I was there for eleven months and I had nothing else to eat in all that time. People died and then were taken away.

The worst moments were the beatings – they were the worst. Everyone was beaten. We kept going because we were convinced about the cause; all our lives were devoted to the fight against Fascism.

We tried to keep our spirits up – we sang songs, even Spanish and Russian songs. Certainly we had thoughts about escaping but we saw what happened to the German anti-Fascist members of the brigades who had tried to get away. They were caught, beaten mercilessly, thrown into solitary confinement and fed starvation rations. Our hearts bled for them. The dungeon they were kept in was small and its only windows were boarded up and they were left in complete darkness. They were only allowed out once a day to relieve themselves. Several prisoners died. When they were seriously ill, they were taken to a so-called hospital, run by nuns, which was part of the prison camp. We would never see them after that – the next thing we'd be told was that they had died.

We all hated Franco before we went to Spain, but in the prison we felt it even more so. There were four of us Irish together in the prison – there were other Irish, but they didn't have the guts to admit they were Irish.

We established an underground committee and began to organise the 'San Pedro Institute of Higher Education' to maintain our dignity and show the Fascists our level of culture, which they despised. We grouped ourselves into different classes – maths, music, languages and so on.

The Americans put on a play about Hiawatha, but it didn't get much further than 'Is that your man-child, Dropping Water?' before everyone burst out laughing at the sight of the 'squaw' walking in with straw wrapped in dirty rags as the 'child'. There was more basic entertainment, too: some of the Americans, who'd got hold of a candle, held farting competitions to blow it out.

Mouse racing was another diversion. I could feel them at night, running across my blanket. I used my tin plate to catch them, setting it at an angle against the wall next to my head with a sardine as bait. When I heard a mouse, I'd slam the plate against the wall, trapping it. Next day we would tie a long thread to their tails and lower them out of the window onto the patio to race.

A month after our capture we had a visit from a Colonel Martin, who seemed to be acting as some kind of representative of the British Government. We told him of the beatings, starvation and vermin, but he was only interested in knowing who in England was responsible for our recruitment. He threatened that, if we didn't tell him, there would be no possibility of an exchange. We refused his demands – we knew he wanted the information in order to prosecute individuals and organisations in Britain for supposedly breaching the non-intervention policy. Not one of more than a hundred British and Irish prisoners acceded to his demands.

We had among us a couple of collaborators who, when captured, quickly gave the Fascist salute. From then on they acted as agents for the Fascists within the camp. We swore that if we returned home we would endeavour to kill them or throw them overboard. They became *cuartaleros* – prison guards – and collaborated in every way with the Fascists. They even asked to be transferred because they didn't want to mix with the reds.

More frequent visitors were two members of the Gestapo. Dressed in civvies they would drive up from Burgos in a Mercedes and interrogate all the international prisoners. We were not as frightened of them as the German prisoners were. When I was brought before them, they showed me several blown-up photographs – a long wooden table with empty wine bottles, spent candles and bits of arms and other human remains. 'Look at these!' they said. 'What do you think? Terrible! You did it!'

They asked, 'Why did you come to Spain?'

I replied, 'I'm an Irish Republican. I came to defend the Republican Government.'

One of them measured me, while the other jotted down the readings – everything about me *athletisch* [athletic]. Then I was photographed naked. The object was to prove that we were subhuman. Our treatment as prisoners was a deliberate strategy to demoralise us and make out that we were sub-human, and could not be normal to have come and fought in the International Brigades.

On Sunday 12 June 1938 Frank Ryan was taken away by three guards. He told us he thought he was going home and was in good form. Johnny Lemon and I gave him notes to take back to Ireland and post. It was a sunny day. An American Jeep came and Frank got into it. There were two guards and he wasn't handcuffed. We watched out of the window as he was driven away. When the last Brigaders were repatriated, the only Irishman left behind was Frank Ryan. Only later did I learn that he had been taken to Burgos jail and sentenced to death.

Some time later, all the prisoners were taken out to a wood and filmed, with all the 'non-Aryans and Jews' placed nearest the camera. We had few clothes because they took our good clothes and boots off us when we were captured. I had no trousers, for example, and only wore a bit of blanket around me. Photos appeared in the *Diario de Burgos*, which was shown to us in jail, with the caption 'Russians captured on the Aragón front'.

Six months after our arrival in San Pedro, the first week of September 1938, we were surprised when all prisoners received a khaki shirt, a pair of breeches and canvas shoes. We wondered what was happening and learnt that we were to receive an 'important visitor'. It turned out to be Lady Chamberlain, widow of the British Foreign Secretary, Austen Chamberlain, who was the brother of the Prime Minister, Neville Chamberlain. She was accompanied by a lordly looking type, complete with monocle, cane and spats.

The British and Irish were lined up for a rehearsal of 'Rompen Filas!' and to make sure we hadn't forgotten the Franco salute. The retinue emerged from the commander's office, and Lady Chamberlain inspected the line of prisoners, asking why they had come to Spain. Everyone replied, 'To stop Fascism before it comes to England.' This was not the answer she wanted. Presumably she would have preferred someone to say, 'I was in Hyde Park one day and someone came up and asked me if I wanted to go to Spain. As I was unemployed, I joined up.'

Disgusted with the replies, she turned to her escort and said, 'I say, can you pick me out an intelligent one?'

However, her visit brought us some comfort. We received our first bit of greens that day – three lettuce leaves with our beans – a welcome sight for all those already suffering from scurvy.

We established that Colonel Martin was the British military attaché in Burgos. He confirmed that negotiations for possible exchange were under way. We had heard that the Italians wanted five artillerymen for each of the International Brigaders. We felt proud of our exchange value for each Fascist.

Christmas 1938 was approaching. The beatings got less and we were even taken to a river and given a bar of soap to bathe. The river had a few deep pools, and it was our greatest treat – the prisoners, all naked, splashing around in full view of the local peasant women pounding their clothes, while our guards kept watch. It was pathetic to see the prisoners with their shirts off, cracking the fat lice between thumb and finger which had penetrated every crevice of their clothing.

Christmas was an historic event. The nine months of terror against us had failed to break our spirit. A number of prisoners had died under the strain, but we managed to maintain our morale despite the Fascists' attempts to demoralise us. The committee had decided to celebrate Christmas by holding a concert, and coordinating the efforts of all the groups who had been attending the various classes. We were determined to show our persecutors that we had culture, and inwardly hoped that our efforts would result in a better climate and reduce the beatings.

The commander's initial ban on our rehearsals was lifted after it was agreed that no revolutionary songs would be performed. We were delighted and invited him and his officers to attend the performance. On Christmas Eve we were surprised to see him crossing the patio with a group of officers and men. We were even more delighted to see that they carried no arms or sticks.

We showed our guests to the front seats, made up from our sleeping bags of straw. Filthy blankets hung on a wire comprised the curtain, decorated with several silver three-pointed stars – the International Brigades' symbol with three points, representing the Popular Front uniting liberals, Socialists and Marxists against Fascism.

Our guests, oblivious of their significance, ignored them. The prisoners sat on similar sacks of straw, packing the room from wall to wall. The atmosphere was tense as our MC greeted the commander and his men with the words 'We are happy that you have come to celebrate this Christmas Eve with us.' The programme was truly international – carols and folk songs from Germany, Poland, Italy and Slavonic countries, Cuba, England and the US.

The show began with the eight German prisoners, who astounded our jailers with their rendition of 'Stille Nacht' and 'O Tannenbaum', after which the audience burst into a round of applause, and 'Olé! Olé!', which could be heard all over San Pedro. In the grimness of our surroundings it was impossible to forget that these same Germans had suffered more than anyone from the wrath of the Fascists and Gestapo, and faced a bleak future – even death.

The Germans were followed by all the other nationalities, each making their unique contribution. *The Barber of Seville*, performed with the crudest of props, brought roars of laughter. The Cubans put on a cabaret with some of them dressed as women – they minced across the stage to the applause and delight of the prisoners and guests. We all wondered how they had managed to get hold of the women's clothes.

The climax of the three-hour concert was reached with Rudi Kampt and his eighty-strong choir, consisting of every nation in Europe and the USA. Absolute silence prevailed within the three-foot-thick walls and the dimly lit room as, with perfect clarity, the voices penetrated the adjoining building where the Spanish prisoners were held. It was as if the singers were pouring their hearts and souls into every note in rebellion against their inhuman treatment.

The whole audience rose to its feet, clapping and cheering wildly. Even our jailers stood and joined in the applause. The commander, an old professional soldier, was overheard to remark, 'And these are our prisoners who can sing like this.' He requested a further performance, promising to bring officers from Burgos – to which we readily agreed. We had broken the barrier. We felt we had proved the superiority of our culture and philosophy against that of the German minister Goering, who is supposed to have said, 'When I hear the word "culture", I reach for my gun.'

For weeks life became a bit easier. Things got better on the vermin front, too – as one of the performers, Carl Geiser, said, 'Many of the fleas and lice left us after each performance to establish new residences with our guests.'

After eleven months, news finally came through that we were to be exchanged. We were transferred from San Pedro to San Sebastián, where we were paraded round the plaza. People began to gather on the pavements in response to a loudspeaker blaring out, 'Spaniards! Come and see these criminals who came to fight against the Spanish people!'

We certainly must have looked a desperately decrepit bunch. We were afraid that this was an incitement to get us attacked, so that Franco could mount a propaganda scoop in the international press and claim it was the 'wrath of the Spanish people'. So we decided that the healthiest among us would march at the front, heads held high, in as disciplined a fashion as we could muster. The Fascist officer in front, noticing our change of mood, ordered us to slow down in the hope that our ranks would be thrown into disarray. Suddenly people moved towards us and began pressing chocolate bars and cigarettes into our hands. The Fascists were furious and ordered us to march quickly to the prison.

Ondarreta was a real jail – not like the improvised concentration camp at San Pedro. The prison no longer exists – it appears that the Fascists feared it would become a place of pilgrimage. We found out that four thousand were executed here. When we were taken out for exercise, we saw a firing line in the yard and one of the walls practically cut in two with the bullet and machine-gun marks. Of course, we rushed over to look at them, and, as we did, the Fascists rushed at us with sticks to keep us moving around.

The twenty-six Basque priests here, who were held in solitary confinement, were those who refused to stand up in the pulpit and denounce 'the destruction of Guernica by Republican planes' when the world knew it was the Germans who were responsible for that genocide and destruction. My abiding memory of those priests is the sight of the last two of them, who bade us farewell with a clenched fist at their side. We couldn't salute them back, but we indicated our understanding in our common language.

We were eventually taken to Hendaya where we were deloused, given a shower, a pair of dungarees and had our hair shaved. After this we were taken by the Spanish Civil Guard to the border and handed over to the French gendarmerie. We three Irish were put on the rear of a train with a gendarme, and travelled under guard to Paris, where we were taken to the Irish Consul. He tried to make us sign a statement saying we would pay for our fare from Spain to Dublin; this we refused to do. He then asked us to sign on behalf of our parents, so that they would foot the bill. Again we refused, stating that we hadn't asked to be taken out of Spain, and would be quite happy to go back to join the Republican forces. Reluctantly, he gave us a ticket to Dublin via London.

We arrived in London with only some French money at

6 am, but cabbies recognised us from the other Brigaders who had arrived the day before. They paid for a great breakfast for us. During our stopover we were kitted out with a new suit of clothes, courtesy of the Co-op.

I have been back to Spain and on one of the visits I stamped on Franco's grave. Well, I have outlived him and most of the Fascists against whom I fought.

I am kept going by my favourite quotation from the Russian writer Nikolai Ostrovsky: 'Man's dearest possession is life, and since it is given to him to live but once, he should live as to have no torturing regrets so that when dying he can say, all my strength was given for the finest cause in the world, the liberation of mankind.'

SAM
LESSER

Born 19 March 1918 in the East End of London

I grew up in Hackney, in the East End of London, where increasingly there was a presence of Mosley and the Blackshirts – but, even before then, some of the history of that time was passing by my front door. This was a period of mass unemployment, of out-of-work miners from South Wales singing in the streets and begging. We were quite near Victoria Park, which was like a miniature Hyde Park in that Hyde Park had its Speaker's Corner, and in Victoria Park every Sunday there were similar groups of political people standing up and speaking. As a kid, I would stand there by the bandstand and listen to them. I'd got a scholarship at that time – I hadn't passed my 11+, but in the end I'd got to a secondary school in the east of London, at a place called George Green's. This was in the heart of Poplar, and the parents of most of the kids there were working in the docks or in the shipyards or ship-repair yards in one way or another. It was called George Green's because it was one of the ship-repair companies in the building there. The teachers at the school were also very left-wing in their politics, although they weren't signed-up members of the Communist Party or even of the Labour Party.

During the General Strike in 1926, Victoria Park was closed down and taken over by the military. The army came in with light tanks that were sent down in order to defend the docks against the strikers – so they said. But it was totally unnecessary.

In about 1934 I won another scholarship from my secondary school in London and went to University College, London, in Gower Street. I was just eighteen, and, like many people of my age at that time, I wasn't too certain what I wanted to study, but I decided to go in generally for history; but I got rather fed up with that and switched to, of all things, Egyptology.

Egyptology at University College was outstanding, because it was the only Egyptology department in London – and the biggest in the country at the time. It was headed by Professor Flinders Petrie, who was the outstanding character in British excavation in Egypt. I worked hard and decided, when I finished my course, to go on a dig which was being organised by Petrie during the summer vacation in 1936.

When I went up to the college I was still living at home, and by then I was already politically very much on the left. But when I went up to college, one of the things I got interested in was the OTC – the Officers' Training Corps. Anybody could join if they wanted, but no one was compelled to do so. I was rather fascinated by it – what was it all about?

Why should I, already a bit of a bolshie, want to join an organisation like that? I thought it would be interesting to see how it worked and to learn how to fire a gun – that's why I joined. We had instructors there from either the Grenadier Guards or Coldstream Guards who had garrisons in London – and it wasn't a joke. When you joined, you undertook to attend skilled instruction and take examinations from time to time, which I took and passed. During the vacations, whether it was Easter or summer, we went to firing practice down at Princes Risborough, where I became acquainted with the local beer called Colne Spring, which really knocked you back!

In the summer vacation not only the University of London OTC but similar OTCs from all over the country would come there – and it had a certain cachet – the Commander-in-Chief of the OTC was Queen Mary's brother, the Earl of Athlone. After one particular examination – which I passed – the sergeant major of the Grenadier Guards, who was our chief instructor, came to me and asked if I was interested in carrying on. I asked what he was offering and he said that, during the next vacation, a number of selected people who had passed the examination would be going down to Dover Castle for two or three weeks' training with their junior officers. Was I interested? I said, yes, I'd go. At least I knew my board and lodging would be paid for.

So I did this attachment with a battalion of the Royal Scots at Dover Castle, and a sergeant major of the Grenadier Guards told me I'd done very well and asked if I'd care to join the Supplementary Reserve. I asked what that was, and he said, 'Well, it's a Supplementary Reserve of Officers – you'd do the same sort of training, not as detailed as you do now, take part in the annual camps, and, in the event of war coming, you would be called up on the first day of war being declared.'

I came back to London and started getting ready to go to Egypt on this dig, but then the Spanish Civil War broke out. I had been following the situation – I knew that there had been elections in February of 1936 where the Popular Front government had been elected, and I knew that there were generals who had rebelled against the legally elected government. This Popular Front consisted not only of left-wing parties, but of factions we didn't have in England, such as the left-Republicans who were far removed from the left, and the Communist Party, which was then very, very small. I met some of my friends while I was getting ready to go to Egypt, and we got talking about Spain.

By that time the Fascist threat in Britain was no joke. The Blackshirts held marches in the East End of London and I went with some other students to a couple of their rallies – particularly the ones in the Albert Hall and at Olympia – where there was quite a punch-up. Not only that, but there were some students at University College who had joined the Blackshirts and started turning up to lectures wearing their black shirts – until the Provost of University College banned it. There was no doubt about it: there was a strong anti-Semitic element to their propaganda, in which Mosley in person played a strong part. Coming from a Jewish family myself, I was suddenly alerted to what was going on – and now it wasn't just something that was happening solely in Germany. It was happening here, on our own doorstep.

I talked about this with a couple of my fellow students who had recently joined the Communist Party and who had heard that there were people in Spain – British people – who were already involved in the fighting in Barcelona when the battle started. These people had been in Spain quite by chance, because at that time the world was preparing for the Olympic Games, which were taking place in Berlin. A lot of people thought this was going to be propaganda for Hitler. So they formed a movement to organise what was called a Workers' Olympiad in Barcelona, so there were people going to Barcelona, including those from Britain, preparing for this Workers' Olympiad. When Franco's uprising began, workers' militias had started defending themselves and, particularly in Barcelona, attacking the army barracks, and among them were some English people. At that time there was no talk of anything like International Brigades.

Eventually, after a lot of talk, I decided that, instead of going to Egypt I would go to Spain, and discovered that the Communist Party, while not actually organising it, could help people who wanted to go. One of the things you'd got when you were in the OTC was uniform – made to measure, as we were future officers – and I thought they'd probably be a bit disorganised without uniform so I decided to go in my own. I didn't do this openly – I put my uniform on and over that I put some corduroy trousers and a pullover. My fellow students held a little collection for me and kept asking me what they should buy me. By that time there were rumours going around that Franco was using gas, so they decided that with the money they collected they would go down to the Army and Navy store and buy me a gas mask, "officers: for the use of". So I got this gas mask.

I'd only been abroad once, when I went to Paris a couple of years before, but I had a passport. I got in contact with the Communist Party and this chap who was organising it gave me £10 to buy a ticket to Paris, and an address to go to when I got there. So I kitted myself out – didn't say a word to my parents about this, just to my younger brother who was sworn to secrecy – and off I went across the Channel from Newhaven to Dieppe. In those days when you crossed the Channel from Newhaven to Dieppe the train was rolled onto the ferry.

I went to Paris, met the contact there and hung around a bit. At that time in France there was a very strong movement in support of the Spanish Republic – the French, too, had formed their own Popular Front, and had an election in which the Popular Front won a majority with the Socialists and the Communists and part of the Radical Party, as it was called at the time.

We were put up in a working-class part of Paris and were told to keep our purpose very, very secret. But none of it seemed very secret to me – everybody was going around shouting, *'Les avions pour l' Espagne'*, and other slogans. We were told to go to the Gare de Lyon where I got the train to Perpignan, it seemed to me that everybody was going to Spain to fight – despite it all being so secret.

On the way down, along the route, there were people working on the railway line giving us the clenched-fist salute, calling out, *'Les avions pour l'Espagne'*. At that time, at the very beginning – about September, October – anybody could go to Spain. We were told we'd be put on buses and coaches to cross the frontier – if anybody stopped us and asked who we were or where we were going, we were to say we were Spanish workers going back to Spain from holiday. As it turned out, we just went in, no problem, and each of us was given a Spanish name, which we were to give if asked. Curiously enough, I still remember that name. It was Raimondo Casado, which also means 'married'. So when we crossed the border into Spain, the picture changed completely. In France people were mixed in their support, but we were there for the Government and the fight against Fascism.

We were sent to a castle in Figueres, which was the first big town on the Spanish side, and from there taken by train to Barcelona, where we stayed a few days. We found the whole place in a ferment of people marching, demonstrating in support of the Republic and against Fascism – and then the train took us to Albacete, which had been chosen as the HQ of what had become the International Brigades – although it hadn't been officially recognised by Government decree until the beginning of October. We did our training there – such as we had. It was at that time we met up with the rest of the British volunteers who had arrived there by one means or another – there were just over thirty of us. We immediately ran into the problem – a core problem for the International Brigades – which was, quite simply, the language. Here you had people from different countries, different nationalities speaking their own languages, and as we British were one of the smallest groups, we were put into a French battalion and training began.

Among this first group were a number of students, paticularly from Cambridge: John Cornford (who was later killed on the Córdoba Front, where I was wounded) and Bernard Knox, who later became a professor of ancient Greek history in the USA. There were a number of people who had been in the British Army, too. This was not a conscript army – there was no conscription or military service in Britain at the time – instead, these were mostly from Scottish regiments, such as the Argyll and Sutherland Highlanders. One of these was a man called Jock Cunningham, who became a very good friend of mine – in fact, he saved my life during the battle for Córdoba after I was wounded – and there were a couple of others from the Black Watch, who certainly knew the way the British army worked.

In training we ran up against the most disgraceful betrayal of democracy in Spain – a betrayal that was headed by the then British Government, under Neville Chamberlain. He became infamous for the policy of appeasement to Hitler and his growing threat of Fascism throughout Europe and the world. Chamberlain came up with this idea of 'non-intervention'– which could be summed up quite simply as 'We don't want Britain involved in this war'. I could well understand those men who had survived the First World War and the massacres of the Somme and Passchendaele, which I had heard so much about as a child; there were families who had lost men and who had wanted to avoid another war at any cost. But the result of this so-called non-intervention policy, as far as Spain was concerned, was to deprive the legally elected government of the Republic of its right, under international law, to purchase arms.

Right away, when we started training, we discovered what non-intervention meant. At first a lot of the training was done with sticks, then one day we were told arms were going to be arriving. An enormous number of cases arrived and our job was to open them up. We found they contained rifles that had been used by the Austrian army in the 1870s, which had been very carefully packed and, to avoid rusting, were covered in grease. The first thing we had to do was to get rid of this damned grease – and the only way you could do it was by getting gallons and gallons of boiling hot water and pouring it through, time and time again. We opened case after case – and you can imagine us, up to our arms with grease all over us – and some people were already expressing doubts as to whether these things would be any damned use, even when we got the grease off. We got the grease off – but where was the bloody ammunition? Everyone was looking for the ammo and then we came across some more cases, opened them up and found the ammo. We discovered that the cartridges in the clips were already green where they had rotted, but we thought we could clean them up and put them through. Once we started trying to fire them, what happened in a number of cases was that the charge would explode in the barrel. You got the kickback and a number of people really didn't look very nice once they'd taken a few of those. So you had to check each individual cartridge to see whether it was wriggling in the clip or not – and that was how we started out.

We thought we were very lucky – at least we had guns, of a sort – but they turned out in many cases to pose a greater danger to us than to the enemy. What was even more dangerous was the matter of hand grenades. Now, to prime a hand grenade you take it in your hand, being careful to hold it so that the pin doesn't spring out – and then you pull the pin and throw it. But there were many Spanish soldiers who had modelled themselves on the miners of the Asturias and how they threw hand grenades. These were very, very brave men and very clever in using explosives in the coal mines. They used explosives to make their own hand grenades, the main process of which was to pack explosive into a tin or something similar with a long piece of wick. You lit it with your lighter, waited until it was burning and then threw it. Some people got so fascinated by watching it burn that the damn thing exploded, and people didn't look very funny if they were caught when these things went off.

So there we were, with all this assorted kit – but at least they were real weapons – and we started drilling. As we were in a

French battalion, all orders were in French – but we were told orders were going to be issued in Spanish, so we had to start learning Spanish too. I'd learnt French and Latin at school, as had some of the others who'd been students, but it was tough going. All the same, things seemed to be going all right. We were training intensively, then one night word went round that training had to stop because the Fascists had broken through the Madrid Front. This was the first time we had heard of anything called a 'front'.

We had to pack up everything overnight, then we were put onto trucks and then on a train. No one told us where it was going, but it was heading for the Madrid Front and we travelled during the night, arriving at the North Station in the early hours of the morning. We detrained and lined up, awaiting orders. This was one of the first battalions of the First International Brigade, which was called the 11th Brigade. You had the French Battalion, which included the French, Belgians, the small group of us British – thirty-five or so – then there was a German Battalion, including some Austrians. The Germans were mostly refugees who had escaped from Hitler's Germany. And there was a Polish Battalion, consisting mainly of Poles who had left Poland years before and who had been working in the coal mines of France. There was a strong anti-Fascist element among them and understandably, right through the war, the French formed the major part of the volunteers in the International Brigades as they were the nearest country.

We British were generally at a disadvantage because we had

no military conscription, whereas in Europe everybody had to go through military service – some for a year or eighteen months, some two years – so they were significantly better trained than we were. It was a question of discipline first of all, of marching around and obeying orders. At that time a number of people, including the Spaniards – and particularly the anarchist element among them – had the feeling that this aspect of military discipline was a waste of time.

We were lined up in Madrid and marched through the city streets, where the crowds, thinking that we must be Russians, were calling out *'son rusos'*, but after a while they realised we weren't. Then we were put into trucks and taken to the Madrid Front, which was the Casa de Campo and University City.

My first impression of Madrid was what a lovely town it was – but already it was a town equipping itself to fight against the Fascists. At the beginning, around November, December 1936, the population was at risk, and large numbers of people were being evacuated – a process which was then accelerated.

University City was an area that had been completely rebuilt with funds provided by one of Franco's most wealthy and fanatical millionaire supporters. The new buildings were really beautiful – and this was where the fighting had begun. The Fascists had advanced at considerable speed through the centre of Spain, and here again we saw how so-called 'non-intervention' was working. When Franco raised the flag of the Fascist generals against the legally elected government, he and the generals commanding the Spanish colonies in North Africa had a problem of how to get colonial troops over to the mainland. These highly trained troops had been used to subdue the native peoples of North Africa. They transported them by Italian military transport planes which were placed at the disposal of Franco's forces to bring over these trained units from North Africa to the mainland. This was the first open indication of the support that Mussolini was bringing to Franco – ferrying this massive movement of troops and units from North Africa to Spain. It was later discovered, when the archives of the British Government were opened up, that the British Consul in Spanish North Africa at the time had sent messages to the Foreign Office in London relating his experiences – how he had stood looking out of the window of his own house and seen these North African troops under Spanish command marching openly down to the airport and boarding the planes for Spain. So it couldn't be said that the British Government and Neville Chamberlain didn't know that there was open intervention on Franco's side.

The Fascists had advanced pretty quickly through the centre of Spain, but they were held up at Toledo where the Fascist garrison was under siege. Franco stopped his forces there to try to lift the siege – which he eventually did – then he continued the advance, right to the gates of Madrid, where the battle began in the Casa de Campo and the University City.

People have asked me if I found my training in the OTC very useful. But actually it wasn't, because much of the fighting in that situation was building to building – and the OTC didn't provide that sort of training. Most of our training was done in open country, based upon the experiences of the British army in the First World War. There's a saying that British army generals were experts in fighting the last war, but were not very well prepared for the next one – which has proved to be right.

So we were fighting, upstairs and downstairs, in the University buildings – with considerable casualties. We're talking about November, December 1936, but this was the first occasion that any Republican force had been able to stop Franco's advance. This was not entirely due to the International Brigades. At that time there, there was only one Brigade formed, because the majority of the resistance came from the Spanish army itself – and we were part of the Spanish army. We defended ourselves at the window we were firing from with as many books from the library as we could find, stuffing them in around us. I remember I had the Everyman series around my window. I never thought, when I returned seventy-two years later to the university, that I would be shown a copy of an Everyman book with a bullet hole in it!

The International Brigades were formed by a decree of the Popular Front government as part of the Spanish armed forces, and under the command of the Ministry of Defence. The Brigades included those officers – and there were very few of them – who had remained loyal to their oath of allegiance to the legally elected government of the Republic, and, outstandingly, by a man who was a colonel at the time but was then promoted to the rank of general – General Rojo – who then became Chief of Staff of the Spanish armed forces.

The fighting halted the Fascist advance – but at considerable cost. That was when we got Russian arms for the first time. Stalin seemed to have taken quite a while to make up his mind what to do about the situation in Spain, because the revolt of Franco and his fellow Fascist generals took place on 18 July 1936, and Soviet arms, as far as we were able to discover, did not start coming to Spain until October. During that time the Fascists were able to advance at considerable speed through the centre of Spain and this wasn't just a military advance. Franco halted his army advance on a number of occasions, and people have asked why didn't he advance more quickly, but it's since been proved quite conclusively that Franco's aim was not just to advance against the Government forces, but to destroy any vestiges of those people who had brought this Popular Front government to power. So, in town after town, when the Fascist troops arrived there was a huge massacre of the civilian population. In Badajoz, thousands were taken into the bullring and machine-gunned down. These were ordinary civilians, and notably teachers – the majority of teachers tended to be progressive in their political outlook and supported the Popular Front government. So they were picked out – [also] people who had been elected as members of a local town council, mayors of the cities and towns where the Popular Front had won a victory in the elections. Admittedly, a lot of people say it was six of one and half a dozen of the other, and that the left-wingers were shooting down the Fascists, too.

The fact was that the Fascist generals, in command in every garrison town, had all the arms they needed at their disposal. However, our Russian weapons had begun to arrive, and the first Number 1 Company was formed, equipped with Russian Maxim machine guns – which are water-cooled guns on little wheels. Unfortunately, part of my OTC training had been on just such a British machine gun – but the difference was that the British machine gun was mounted on a tripod. By shifting the lock, you could disconnect the actual gun from the cooling jacket, so one man carried the gun and the other the tripod. The Russian gun functioned in pretty much the same way as the British, except that you had these wheels and this little truck, which you had to slide it off. I found that it looked all right in the Russian films of the time, with troops marching into action, but, when you started pulling this machine gun along, the nose would keep knocking on the uneven ground and it didn't do much good to the sighting business at the other end. Still, it was a machine gun and we used it as best we could. On one occasion our men found they were surrounded and had to fight their way out, and they forgot to disable the gun when they abandoned it. I had been trained never to abandon my weapon – if you were forced to leave it, you removed the lock, essential in the machine gun. If you removed the lock it was useless unless you carried around a suitcase full of spare locks, which was not the case. So, unfortunately, on a number of occasions, our machine guns fell into the hands of the Fascists, who just turned the bloody thing round and opened up on us.

The battle at University City came to a standstill and, of the thirty-six of us British, there were just six of us left. John Cornford had been wounded – not very seriously, as it turned out – but most of the others had been killed. Casualties were heavy throughout the unit but we had established a line. As to us survivors, we were shipped out to Albacete where, during November and December, more and more volunteers had continued to arrive from all parts of the world, including Britain and, most importantly, a considerable number from the United States. One American ship had been torpedoed and a number killed on board before they arrived in Barcelona. Understandably, the British who had arrived crowded round the six of us, asking how it was going and what it was like – and we did our best to explain how it had gone.

Our training started again, but there were problems with accommodating the increasing number of volunteers who had arrived, particularly from the United States, Britain and other parts of Europe. There were also people from Germany who had escaped the Fascist regime, and from other countries of Eastern Europe as well, so we were billeted in villages surrounding Albacete. Understandably, some of the local inhabitants were not too happy about having to put up large numbers of our volunteers. Still, discipline became increasingly important to impose, and the system was established of appointing officers according to how they did in training, and this seemed to work pretty well. The idea was mooted that the British training would continue until a sufficient number of volunteers had arrived to form a British Battalion and that was the objective. So we formed ourselves into companies and the six of us who had survived Madrid were allocated into the different companies. I was sent to Number 1 Company – the machine-gun company.

The area where we were, around Albacete, was in the province of La Mancha – Don Quixote country – and it got blazing hot, especially in the afternoon. We discovered that in the sweltering heat of the afternoon the Spanish would go for their siesta. We also discovered that the main crop that was being cultivated in the fields – and still largely is – was a thing called *azafrán*. This was saffron – an extremely expensive spice which is added to soups and paella. Saffron comes from the crocus and these flowers were cultivated over a large area. The procedure was that in the morning women would go out with sacks and fill them with flowers, and in the afternoon they'd take out the essential part, which is the stamen, and lay them out to dry. The women would sit in the shade, picking over these flowers – and we thought we'd help, and maybe get acquainted with the local population. But we soon discovered that every girl there had an aunt or mother who was keeping a sharp lookout for any funny business. It was a way of getting acquainted – but that wasn't to last too long.

Training was going quite well, and those who had shown initiative were promoted and appointed sergeants, lieu-tenants, and a chain of command was taking shape. Then one night the word went round that the Fascists had broken through on the Córdoba Front, and everybody – cooks, the lot – was taken to the local railway station at Albacete, put on a train and sent across Spain to a place called Andújar, where we detrained.

As we were getting out of the trains we came under attack from the air – machine-gunned from the aircraft – and I remember our first casualty at that time was a man from the East End, who had been at Cable Street – Harry Segal. He was killed as he was getting out. I saw him as he was hit, and his body fell to the ground. That raises another enormous deficiency on the Republican side – the total lack of any proper air force. Already, military transport planes were coming from Italy and also, from Germany, came the planes that became part of the infamous Condor Legion, which later sealed its reputation with the mass attack on the civilian population of Guernica, made famous by Picasso in his painting. People look at it today and begin to understand what Picasso was thinking when he produced this masterpiece.

On the Republican side there were a few planes, but they were few and far between and only later on did the Russians start sending aircraft. The only way Russian equipment could reach Spain was by ship through the Mediterranean, and the Mediterranean was controlled by the German and Italian navies. You may well ask what the British Royal Navy was doing – here was the Royal Navy, which had been built up and had existed for many years, its *raison d'être* being the defence of the route to India, through the Mediterranean and the Suez Canal. One of the most disgraceful aspects of this British-inspired policy of non-intervention was that, time after time, the Royal Navy stood by while the navies of Fascist Germany and Italy patrolled unchallenged. A number of Soviet ships brought machine guns and some artillery, but very little. At that time there was no plane that could have been flown non-stop from the Soviet Union to Spain, whereas from Germany to Spain it was much easier. So, the decision had been taken that the Soviet Union would supply fighter planes. To get these to Spain, the planes had to be dismantled and packaged in Russia, and reassembled in Spain. The question of piloting them was also a problem, but there was a process of selection of youngsters of seventeen, eighteen and nineteen, who had shown themselves to be super-brave in the ordinary hand fighting in the Spanish Republican armed forces. These elite had been selected for training in the Soviet Union for some six months, and when they came back they really were valiant in manning those few planes at their disposal, but all the same the Fascists controlled the air. The Condor Legion demonstrated the German policy of using Spain as a testing ground, and they honed their aerial attacking skills to a fine art.

Incidentally, I met one of the Catalan youngsters who were trained as pilots for the Republican air force, at a commemoration in the Sierra de Pandols in 2006. He was captured eventually, after spending years in the mountains with one of the small groups that resisted Franco well into the 1950s, and imprisoned and tortured. But he's still going strong now in his late 80s!

We underwent more training at Andújar, then went on trucks to the front. There was a very bitter battle at a town called Lopera and, personally, I was not in very good shape although I had survived Madrid, but we advanced there, as ordered.

They decided to gather all the British volunteers who were then at Albacete in various stages of their training and form a company – that's 120–130 men. We were under the command of an Irish comrade who was later killed – a wonderful chap. Of the volunteers that came from the British Isles, a considerable number were Irish. Some of them had got some military experience in the fighting against the British armed forces during 1922 and that period of very stormy relations between Great Britain and the newly formed Irish Republic, and many of them had been in the IRA. If you look through the casualty list of that first fight – the battle for Lopera on the Córdoba Front, you will see, one after another, the names of Irish comrades who fell there.

As we advanced we came under very heavy fire and had to keep our heads down. I did my best, but, not far from me, John Cornford and Ralph Fox were killed. There were heavy casualties and I was wounded. I didn't know at the time where I'd been wounded – in which part of my body – except that when I tried to get up I couldn't. I just fell down – there was something wrong with my legs. As the day progressed, our people had to retreat and I was lying there unable to move – and there was no possibility of a stretcher-bearer coming for me. We were badly equipped, even with the Russian weapons, but particularly in respect of the medical equipment, which was very, very sparse. By that time we had a few doctors and nurses who had come as volunteers to Spain, but the medical equipment was very scarce. Interestingly, a very important part of the mass movement of support for the Spanish Republic throughout Great Britain focused specially on medical aid, including fully fitted-out ambulances and other medical equipment. But at the battle for Córdoba it was very difficult, and while I was lying there I always remember hearing them calling out, in Spanish, for stretcher-bearers to come. I lay there that night in what had become no man's land, because our people had had to withdraw.

It was a long time later that I was told that people started looking for me, and Jock Cunningham, who'd been with the Argyll and Sutherland Highlanders and had become a great friend of mine during the Battle of Madrid, said he was going out and looking for me.

Apparently they said, 'It's no use, Jock, he's a dead 'un, a goner, and if you go out you'll be a goner too.'

Jock, to his credit, said he was going anyway. He looked around and found me – then literally dragged me in, because he couldn't find a stretcher. I had got a bullet in my left leg, and also in my back – because I had an early encounter with what in the Second World War came to be called 'friendly fire'. Our French comrades, who were on our right flank to support our advance, were sending over crossfire. We had apparently advanced too quickly and when they saw us they opened fire.

I was dragged by Jock and finally dropped on a stretcher and taken clear of where the fighting was still going on. Then we discovered another aspect of the shortages we'd been labouring under. First, there was the difficulty of finding a stretcher and then an ambulance or some way of getting the wounded clear of the fighting. I was put into an agricultural cart and, by God, it stank to high heaven – you could tell what it had been used for before. I finally got clear of the lines and we wounded were put into trucks – not ambulances – there was no such thing as an ambulance there. The walking wounded were sitting as best they could in the truck, stretchers were put where they could be fitted in and we were driven to a place, part of which is now a large town called Linares.

We were unloaded from these trucks at what we were told was a hospital. During the night large numbers of the town's population kept coming in, and, as we were being unloaded from the trucks, they were clapping and cheering us. But that was nothing compared to what happened the following morning. When it got light, the hospital was absolutely stormed by people coming up from the town. These people had brought everything they could think of – ordinary things like soap and toothbrushes and toothpaste and packets of pastries and bottles of wine. Everybody wanted to shake our hands and say thank you.

These were ordinary, poor people, and even a small thing like a toothbrush was beyond their means, but they felt that we were there for them, so they wanted to thank us for joining their cause and fighting on their behalf.

This hospital was, like so many hospitals in Spain at the time, run by a religious order. All the nurses were nuns – Sisters of Mercy. Perhaps they weren't as well trained as British nurses, but they did the best they could, and there were a number of doctors there, too. The main problem, at least for me, was that, it being a religious institution, they kept ringing bells all the time. Naturally, in Spain, in a Catholic institution, there were summons to prayer throughout the day. Many of the wounded who survived ended up together in this hospital in Linares. Some of them were walking wounded and when they'd been treated they volunteered to rejoin the unit in Albacete.

My wound was not that serious, but with the limitations of the medicines there it began to get infected, and my leg was not plastered but bandaged up. There again, even the simple things like bandages were always in short supply and, of course, this was before antibiotics – streptomycin or sulphonamides – and the medical supplies were very restricted. Finally I recovered sufficiently and I said that I wanted to go back to the front. I still had to have the wound dressed but they finally agreed that I could go back to Albacete and work there. Each national unit in the International Brigades had an officer there, and the British Battalion office was under the command of Peter Kerrigan.

I worked there doing a lot of paperwork. There were new volunteers arriving all the time, and there were records that had to be kept – information about casualties from the front. I worked pretty hard there, while at the same time being able to get my wound attended to. But the battle continued, and the Fascists, at first held up in the Casa de Campo in Madrid and then on the Córdoba Front, had managed to open up another front in what came to be the first big battle of that war – the Battle of Jarama.

By the time the Battle of Jarama developed, the British Battalion had been formed. There were roughly six hundred men under a proper commander with a proper chain of command, in what became the English-speaking brigade of the International Brigades – that is including the Americans, the Canadians and others. Working in the office in Albacete, we began to get information about how the battle was going – and it was a battle! Then one day we got the first casualty list and I shall always remember when we opened it. We had a messenger who had come to Albacete with these casualty lists, and we knew there had been very heavy fighting, but we were absolutely horrified when we saw this casualty list. I remember talking over with Kerrigan what we were going to do – how to get this information to London. Unlike the British army, we didn't have lines of communication and offices in place, and the problem was how to convey news of those killed or wounded to their families.

It was the opinion of the doctors in Albacete that I should go back to London for proper medical treatment, and I should take the casualty list back with me. I had my passport, so there was no problem there, and no difficulties at the French frontier, so when I got to London I handed over the information, and the organisation, such as it was in London, had to inform the families.

By that time the movement in England in support of Spain had widened enormously, particularly among doctors and nurses, including, among the nurses, a young Welsh woman, Margaret Powell who later became my wife. Arrangements were made for me to go and see a top orthopaedic man in Harley Street, Lord Horder, who had me taken to the Hammersmith Hospital. The actual wound was not that bad, but in later life my foot gave me quite a lot of trouble – but I was very lucky and consider I got off quite lightly. As soon as I started working within the organisation in London, Aid for Spain, I wanted to get back to the Front. In the end it was decided I should go to work in Paris, organising the volunteers from different parts of the world – meeting them from the train when they came in, taking them to places where they could stay overnight.

Every unit in Spain, made up of all the different national-ities, was named after some outstanding person in their particular country, starting with the French. They didn't have to look very far; there were a number of French battalions as the number of French volunteers increased, so one battalion took the name The Marseillaise and another was called the Commune de Paris. But the Italians – and there were quite a large number of anti-Fascist Italians who, like the Germans, had been living and working in France – called themselves the Garibaldis. The Germans called themselves the Thaelmann Battalion, after the leader of the German Communist Party, and the Poles called themselves the Dombrovsky Battalion. However, nobody could decide what we should call the British. So someone said they'd call it the Saklatvala and we said, 'Who's he?' He turned out to be an Indian who had been elected as a Labour MP for Battersea, and, after he'd been elected, he announced that he would be a Communist from then on. But among the first militias that had been formed among the people who had come to Barcelona to take part in the Workers' Olympiad, they'd given themselves the name the Tom Mann Militia. Tom Mann was a famous leader of the dockers in London, where there had been great battles and strikes to try to end the system of casual labour in the docks, by which individuals were selected for work each day. However, Saklatvala just didn't fit and in the end we were simply called the British Battalion. But there were a lot of the Irish who were not at all happy about that and actually at one stage a number of the Irish who had come to Spain to fight for the Republic said they weren't going to be part of a bloody British Battalion! Some of them actually had left, demanded the right to leave, and went to join the first American units. There was a Lincoln and a Washington Battalion as their numbers increased, but after their heavy casualties at Jarama they were joined into one and called the Lincoln-Washington Battalion. They later called themselves the Lincoln Brigade, although in strict military terms they were never enough to form a whole brigade, which should have been at least three battalions – about 1,800 men. We were called the British Battalion or as the French would call them 'Les British' or 'Les Anglais'. Of course, when you called them 'Les Anglais', the Scots didn't like to be called English.

I was in Paris working on the line and helping in any way I could, and we were getting people coming through Paris who had been wounded and were being repatriated to England. I was beginning to get agitated – I wanted to go back to Spain – and in the end, after a lot of argument with our French comrades, they sent me to Perpignan, where I was told that there were a number of young women from different parts of Europe who had reached France and wanted to go to Spain. There were no British among them at all, because the movement of British nurses to go to Spain had been started quite independently of those who were going to Spain to fight in the International Brigades. There was a Spanish Medical Aid Committee set up, and they were properly organised with the help of the TUC. There were a number of nurses and doctors – too few, but what they did was pretty marvellous. They were under the direct command of the Ministry of Defence Medical Department and served wonderfully in various units. Today one of those nurses is still with us – Penny Feiwel – a wonderful woman.

They told me in Perpignan that these women couldn't get to Spain the way the men were getting in, doing the hike across the Pyrenees, so another way was devised. There was a fisherman who had his own boat, and the plan was to go from a small fishing village on the French side, take them by night and then land them on the Spanish side. I was to be in charge of this operation.

First, I had to collect these young women from various addresses in Narbonne, Carcassonne, and Montpellier and bring them to Perpignan. When I was told all this I was a bit surprised, and when they handed me two tickets in Paris, I asked, 'Why do I need two tickets?'

'Well, there's a young woman going down there, and you're to take her with you.'

I was introduced to this young lady who was Polish, and didn't speak anything except Polish. I didn't speak any Polish. I said, 'Let's go to the station.'

But she kept saying, '*Apteka, Apteka*', and I couldn't think what the hell she was talking about.

Then I finally thought, 'Apotheke' – that must be a chemist. I spotted a pharmacy. We went in – and I thought this young woman probably wanted something from the chemist that a young fellow like me wouldn't know about. So while she was chatting to the chemist, she kept saying '*Enna Perska*'. She wanted henna for her hair – and it had to be Persian henna. This was my first experience of the perfidiousness of women! Here we were, going to help the Spanish Republic, and this woman wanted to buy henna. Anyway, off we went, and I delivered her to Perpignan.

We got these twelve or fifteen women together and one Sunday afternoon in July we got in a bus and went down to this small village called Agde – which was a tiny place. We got these women on board, and a French chap arrived with an enormous tin of tuna, bread, butter and wine. We travelled all night, and at times some of the girls got very alarmed in case there were Royal Navy patrols. However, we made it through and I handed over my crew. I then went on to Barcelona, where I was ordered to join the International Brigades. They said I must go for a medical examination and they decided I was not fit for front-line service. Instead, I was given an address to go to, and, as I arrived, a man said, 'We've been waiting for you.'

It turned out that this was the headquarters set up by the Spanish to broadcast on short wave, in German, Italian, Portuguese and English, and I was going to be in charge of the English-language broadcasts.

I said, 'I've never done anything like this before.'

But they said, 'You'll find out. We'll take you to your room – there's your typewriter . . .'

I said I'd seen typewriters before, but never used one.

All they said was 'Your broadcast is at seven o'clock, for half an hour every night, and you are on tonight.'

I said, 'How can I?'

But they said, 'See those papers there? You'll find some things that your predecessor – who has returned to England – has prepared. You can use that.'

That's how I became a journalist – I lost all idea of going to Egypt and began a career as a journalist.

I began to meet a lot of reporters such as Geoffrey Cox, who became Head of Yorkshire Television. He was a correspondent for the *Daily Express*, and Sefton Delmar was with the *Daily Express* at one time. There was also William Forrest of the *News Chronicle*, and Herbert Matthews of the *New York Times* – he'd been a correspondent for some time and had reported on the war in Abyssinia, on the Italian Fascist troops there. He'd done it so well, so Mussolini thought, that he decorated him for his work. One day I was talking with the woman who was in charge of Foreign Press department of the Spanish Foreign Ministry and she said that Herbert Matthews was coming to Barcelona. Matthews became one of the most ardent supporters of the Republic and reported what was happening in Spain. It was only recently discovered that a lot of what he reported was sabotaged by staff in the office of the *New York Times* because they didn't agree with it. His copy was 'spiked' because they had editorial control in the office in New York. Even more interesting was the correspondent for the *Daily Telegraph*, Henry Buckley, an ardent Catholic when he was sent to Spain, who became a staunch supporter of the Republic.

I carried on with these broadcasts, which was very difficult because Barcelona was being bombed. Sometimes people from the British Battalion took some leave in Barcelona and they would look me up. They used to say it was more dangerous there than at the front. The Italians had turned nearby Majorca into an air force base

I shall never forget the night they bombed us. The upper part of Barcelona is laid out geometrically, and the bombing was pretty amateur – they just leaned out and dropped bombs at every crossing that they could see. There were some air-raid shelters but not very many. As in the Second World War in the Blitz, there would be an alert, the bombs would fall and then silence – nothing would happen. You should get the all clear, but people would start coming out of the shelters and looking around, saying, 'The people who were supposed to have sounded the all clear must have forgotten and gone home.' And they'd start wandering around. Then the Fascists would come a second time and drop their bombs.

They bombed our area of Barcelona, and I shall never forget the smell there when I went outside. There was one wonderful row of lime trees – a beautiful scent when they're in flower. But people had come out, particularly from the police station – policemen had come out from their shelter, strolling around – and more bombs had been dropped. The gutter was literally flowing with blood, and the smell of the blood of these poor people mixed with the smell of the lime trees. I carried on, but Barcelona was not an easy place to be, quite apart from the bombs, and my food rations were the same as the ordinary population.

The war continued, the suffering got worse, and in Barcelona the food rationing increased. The bombing intensified, we became very isolated, and I didn't realise how the situation was developing outside Spain. I'd got a woman called Fermina in to help me with the broadcasts as my secretary, and at that time Chamberlain was negotiating with Hitler to draw up the Munich Agreement. There was a lot of talk in our office as to what this agreement would mean. Fermina said, 'It means the end of us.'

I was furious with her. I said, 'How dare you say a thing like that?'

And it was obvious that she was repeating what she had heard from leading people who had discussed the likely effect of the Munich Agreement on Spain. They had come to the conclusion that it would mean the end of the Spanish – which turned out to be true. I carried on being a correspondent, and only got out across the frontier thanks to being given a lift in a car that was run by the *Daily Herald* correspondent Scott Watson. I got out of Barcelona the day before the Fascists entered on 26 January 1939.

Many times I've thought about this – the road to the French frontier was crammed, mostly with women, children and old men trying to get out. It was something that would later be re-enacted in towns in countries across the whole of Europe. Through our fighting in Spain we had been trying in our small way not only to save Spain, but, as I said in this slogan that I think I invented, 'To save peace and to save Britain'. At one stage we couldn't get any further along the road, so Scott Watson got out of the car with his Spanish girlfriend. We walked along this little road, but it was blocked and we couldn't get through. Night had fallen and it was pouring with rain, and as we got nearer the frontier we saw troops manning it on the French side. The French Government, to its eternal disgrace, had sent Senegalese troops under European commanding officers, to man that frontier to stop anyone from getting through. But earlier on I had seen, near the frontier, the defeated remnants of the Spanish army. By that time the International Brigades had been officially withdrawn and the non-intervention committee had appointed a military committee to control the withdrawal of the volunteers. I went there, as correspondent of the *Daily Worker*, with this group of military men, commanded by a British general, who was standing there. All along this road were the remnants of the Spanish Republican army – in tatters, beaten. Some of them hadn't slept for a week. They had to throw down what arms they had, and there were mountains and mountains of discarded guns. There were British officers and some from other countries, and this sticks in my mind: one officer, who turned out to be Persian, was inspecting this growing pile of arms. He was rooting about and picked up a revolver which had a mother-of-pearl handle. He took it to the British general and said, 'What do you think of this?'

And he replied, 'A very nice piece.'

This Persian said, 'Can I have it, General?'

And he said, 'Yes.'

I thought, 'You bastards – here are we, fighting this fight to a standstill, and all you can think about is picking up this thing as a toy for yourself.' But there was nothing I could do.

When we got to the barricade, the Senegalese troops were stopping people from getting through – they just put their hand in your face. There in the darkness, a light came on the other side, and out stepped a man in uniform, a French officer, and he stood there for a bit. We were there talking in

English, trying to get the Senegalese troops to understand –
and he came over and said, 'Excuse me, gentlemen, can I be
of any assistance?' in the sort of accent you could cut with a
knife. We explained our position and he motioned us to his
hut where he signed our passports and put a stamp on them
and we were in France, but the Republicans were left there,
and they suffered dreadfully.

In the end the Republicans were put in what became camps
– but they weren't camps; they were places on the sand, on
the coast where there was nothing – and kept in captivity
there. I didn't know at the time but among those people was
the woman who became my wife. She had been a nurse there,
and had retreated because most of the nurses joined the
English-speaking brigade. But Margaret didn't want to go –
she was working very well with a surgeon in the Spanish
division and when the retreat started she stayed with them,
and did the best she could, having to shift place every night,
to deal with wounded and sick.

Why did I go to Spain? I had the choice of going to Egypt to
do this dig, and I was quite excited about it, but thinking
about it and talking it over with fellow students, or comrades
as they were at that time – some of whom had already joined
the Communist Party – the fight against Fascism became the
number-one priority. This was before the Battle of Cable
Street. By the time Cable Street happened I was already in
Spain. A younger brother of mine who came out to Spain
also took part in the battle at Cable Street and many people
who were there subsequently went to Spain.

What did we hope to achieve? We hoped to ensure that the legally elected government of the Republic would get its proper rights and be recognised internationally. We failed there, no doubt – largely through the machinations of the British Government. We tend to forget nowadays that, at that time, Britain was a leading country in the world and the decisions of the British Government influenced strongly worldwide international politics and international diplomacy.

People say, 'Well, you couldn't have beaten Franco at the time', but I think we could have done, if the British Government had permitted the Spanish Government its rights under international law to purchase arms. The Spanish could have beaten Fascism, and could have stopped Hitler and Mussolini. I know it sounds idiotic to say so – we might even have averted or avoided the Second World War.

Asked if I would do it all again, I used to give an unequivocal reply that of course I would. But now I don't know if I would. I'm a very old man now and one of the things I experienced was that those of us who survived Spain experienced different sorts of treatment when we got back.

It has to be said that, when the end of the Spanish war came in April 1939, the massacre and the butchery carried out by Franco's regime continued until the last day – even to the day Franco died in 1975 – and a reign of terror was established over Spain, so that people dared not speak openly. It was only after Franco's death that another government was elected under a new constitution – a democratic constitution – and people started to say, 'Yes, we know where

they are buried – the people who were shot and massacred.'
And it was not until this present government was elected
under Prime Minister Zapatero, whose own grandfather
had been taken out and shot in the streets, that people began
to speak out and demand the right to give the victims of
that massacre the proper burial – and this is taking place now
in Spain. At the same time the new, legally elected government passed a decree, paying tribute to the work of the
International Brigades and offering Spanish citizenship to
those of us who wanted to take advantage of this – but this
had had to wait for many, many years. And, because of an
error in the decree that was issued at that time, only now has
it been properly established that we have the right to acquire
Spanish citizenship if we choose. It's only recently that
that stipulation has been removed, but time has not stood
still, and unfortunately large numbers of the International
Brigades have gone the way of all flesh and will not be able
to claim their Spanish citizenship – unless some Spanish
Embassy up there will provide it!

LES GIBSON

Born 6 September 1913 in Fulham, west London

I was born in Aspenlea Road in Fulham. There were eight children in my family. I had four brothers and three sisters. We had a small house, and we were overcrowded really, but we got on well. We had two bedrooms, and the way they did it was that Mum slept in one room with the girls and Dad in the other with the boys. There were always two in a bed – snug! My eldest brother went to Fulham Palace Road School, then passed a scholarship and went to Latimer – a very posh school. There he passed a scholarship to go to Cambridge University but he didn't go. He said Dad couldn't afford to keep him until he was twenty-odd, so he went to work for WH Smith.

When I was five it was the end of the First World War. My dad was in the war – he'd been a time-serving regular soldier, and he was an expert gunlayer with the artillery. They made him a sergeant, gave him a team – they were horse-drawn in those days – and sent him straight over to France. I didn't see much of him before he left but the first time he came back in his uniform, and he turned the corner of Aspenlea Road, I ran up to him.

He was a good dad, looked after us very well. We used to go out walking on Sundays if the weather was nice. He'd take us youngsters for a long walk with Mum pushing the pram. We walked to Hammersmith, down the bridge over onto the towpath, along Putney Bridge, then down the steps into Bishop's Park. Then we'd walk right through until we came to the Fulham Football Club ground – Craven Cottage – and we'd walk from there all the way home. That was our short walk. If we wanted a long walk we'd go right down to Barnes Common, over Putney Bridge and home. We didn't eat while we were out, but we did get a fizzy drink outside the pub – ginger beer. In many ways it was a very happy childhood.

Dad just got on with life after the war. When he'd finished his time with the army he started work as a plasterer's mate. He was known in the building trade as Old Harry.

I was five when I went to Fulham Palace Road School. Opposite it there used to be the workhouse with the clock outside – we'd to set our time by that because it would strike and we could hear it. Fulham was a rough area in those days, but the people were all right – I got on with them. When I was six I used to go out delivering Labour Party leaflets down some of the roughest turnings, but it didn't worry me.

When I went to school, my first teacher was Miss Hannibal

and she was very strict. I had several clouts round the ear from her. There were about thirty of us in the class, just five- to six-year-olds. I got to the top class in the school when I was twelve, but what held me back was not being able to get on with my work because I had to go to a clinic to have drops put in my eyes. When that was done I couldn't see – I'd go there on my own, but had a penny for my fare back, and that was a treat in those days because you usually walked everywhere.

I didn't play football at school, although all my brothers did. I was very tall so there was never any bullying for me. I did have a spell of it once – there were four boys who used to gang up on me and punch me, and I didn't fancy the odds at four to one, but my mum saw me when I stripped for a wash. She saw the bruises on me and she wanted to know where they came from. She made me tell her and she went up to the school. I came out from school one day and there was one of these boys – on his own. So I went up to him and said, 'Right, I see you're a big lad when you've got the other three with you – try your luck now.' He finished up lying on the floor. I used to stand up for myself.

I left school in 1927 – but I'd been aware of the General Strike in 1926. My dad didn't work during the strike but it was through my mum's influence that I delivered the leaflets when I was young. My oldest sister – three years older than me – was the secretary of the Labour Youth. She was the founder of it in Fulham, and the lower age for joining was sixteen, but they let me join when I was fourteen because I'd done so much work for the Labour Party. Our MP at the time was Cyril Cobb. As kids we used to get the metal lids off the dustbins outside – because we used to have to put them out the front in those days – and we'd get a stick and march round the street banging on the lid with a stick and singing 'Vote for Mr Gentry' – that was the Labour man – and 'Kick old Cobby out the door'. Cobb was a Conservative.

One day, when I was twelve, I'd been on an errand and when I came back there was a platform set up on the corner of Aspenlea Road. It had a banner on it: 'Conservative meeting at six o'clock'. A crowd started to gather, because it was unusual for Conservatives to speak on street corners, and so I stood by the platform. The speaker was by the chairman, and he got up and made a direct statement. My memory was good so when he made this direct statement, and went on talking, then made another direct statement that was contradictory to the first one, I called out, 'Mr Speaker!' He said, 'Yes, sonny?' – he probably thought, 'We've got a good one here' – and I said, 'When you started your speech, you said . . .' – and I quoted him word for word – 'and now you've said . . .' – and I quoted him again. I said, 'As the truth is never contradictory, which of those statements is true and which is false?'

He said, 'You cheeky little whippersnapper – you haven't got the cradle marks off your arse yet.'

Then a big voice came up and I knew who it was as soon as I heard it – it was my mate's dad, who lived opposite me. He had a great booming voice – a big man. He said, 'Answer the boy – don't insult him!'

And then the whole crowd started up, 'Answer the boy!' The

crowd was getting irritated with him, and started to move in on him.

They had to pack up and go.

I remember two girls from my infant school, Florrie and Rosie particularly, because I liked them. Florrie Windmill was a pretty little girl with naturally curly hair, but Rosie Cash was more of a classical beauty – and I still remember them. In fact, I saw Rosie Cash once again when I was twenty-one – because by that time I was a Co-op milkman. I didn't know where she lived, but I saw her when I pulled up and parked my barrow while I went home for a cup of tea. You see, we did two rounds in those days. You went round first dropping milk at the front steps, because very few people had fridges in those days. In summer especially the milk would go off if they had it too early, so we would go back a second time in case they wanted any more milk. We served it out in bottles, but the sort of milkman was still around where they had a churn and ladled it out.

In 1927 the consequences of the General Strike were still with us, but I managed to get a job. It was somebody else's bad luck really, because a fella broke his arm. I was a paper boy, serving a man who was a buyer for one of the department stores. He said, 'Come and see me when you leave school.' But when I went and saw him, he said, 'Sorry, it's too near Christmas. I can't do anything at the moment.' So I went back to school, but he kept my name and address and when the poultry man wanted a boy quickly he sent for me. But I hated it, poultry cleaning. I could soon bone a chicken out – in fact, there used to be a chef on the TV in the fifties, Philip Harbin, and he would show you how to bone a chicken, cutting down the back, and then stitching it up afterwards. If you'd done that in our day you'd have got the sack. You bone a chicken all through the neck – taking every bone out using a knife.

At twenty-one I was earning thirty bob a week, but that wasn't enough so I tried for a five-bob rise. I worked with Dad as a plasterer's labourer, one of the hardest jobs in the trade. They were building a big factory in Wimbledon for the firm that made Dinky Toy cars. Because of the heavy machinery needed there they had to have a very strong floor – it had to be granite. You had a big gauging box – a square box with no bottom to it – and you filled it up with granite dust. Then you filled it up with granite chippings, and two bags of cement – and you had to mix it twice dry and twice wet. His guv'nor, being in plastering, got the contract for plastering, and the floor laying came under him, too, so he subcontracted to a floor-laying firm, and my dad was helping them lay the floors.

One of the blokes came up to me and said, 'Your old man's a blooming idiot!'

I said, 'Why?'

And he said, 'Being a plasterer's labourer, he's laying the floor as well as we can.'

So I said, 'That's him.' He could lay bricks – he could do anything except plumbing; he wouldn't tackle that. I was very proud of him.

I was a plasterer's labourer for about six months, then I became a chef for this big firm on the Kingston bypass. They were the firm that made the mechanics for the first motor for the slot-machine parking meters. I had to deal with four dining rooms – one each for the directors, the managers and the office staff, then there was the main hall for the factory workers. I got on quite well there. I did this roast chicken which I boned out and stuffed and I sent it in for the guv'nor to carve at the top table. He sent it back out – he didn't know what to do with it. I carved it and sent it back in.

When Ramsay MacDonald became Prime Minister I was in the Labour League of Youth – then eventually Fulham got a Labour MP. I joined the Labour League because I was very left wing, and my eldest brother became a Communist. I was grumbling one day because Ramsay MacDonald had formed the National Party – a national Labour party – and I was saying, 'What are we working for? We're working hard for a bloke who's not interested in doing anything for us. He's interested in keeping his well-paid job.' My brother said to go and talk to Georgie Poole, and sent me to a house off the Shepherds Bush Road, where there were two other lads. One lived there and the other was visiting, and I made up the three – and we became the Young Communist League.

I was a speaker for the Young Communist League, on street corners in the area. On one occasion the Fascists had a meeting on Ealing Common, and so did we, and I'd gone over to their meeting to listen to what they were saying. When I turned to go, they blocked my way so I couldn't get out.

My mates were all over on our area, but when they saw what was happening they came dashing across and they got me out quick – though there was one bloke who tried to stop me leaving. I was unemployed at the time, so I'd been up to sign on. I'd done some work but was out of work for three months – just before Dad got me the job as plasterer's labourer. The one who stopped me from leaving had been walking along by Fulham Cemetery, going up to sign on. I'd already been there and was walking back. When he saw me he ran across the road quick – not that I would have bothered with him. He wanted to get me to join them, but I said, 'Never.'

'Never is a long time,' he said. 'When we take power we'll hang you from the nearest lamp-post.'

And I thought, 'Well, you're simply not going to take power.'

My younger brother and I tried to get through to the big anti-Fascist meeting in London – in Cable Street. We got as far as Oxford Street but the police wouldn't let us go any further. We had to walk all the way home from there – and it was a long walk. We also tried to go to the meeting Mosley held in the Albert Hall. We got our posters and I said to the brigade, 'Put your posters up and put them between the iron railings of the park – don't forget when you get inside, don't try to ask a question if you're on your own. Make sure you've got some-one around you.' We tried to get in and couldn't – evidently we were known.

I'd been the speaker for the last year and we used to have meetings on a Saturday night and Sunday morning in

King Street. When the Spanish Civil War started in 1936, I brought it up at our meetings and said, 'We're supposed to be a democratic country. We're playing a role in this war by stopping Spain from buying arms. It's all right to say "non-interference", but don't forget that, while the government were not allowed to buy arms, the Fascists were getting them all the time – and not only arms, but the men who knew how to use them.'

I didn't tell anyone I had decided to go to Spain – just my brother. I had a friend, Dickie Bird, who left Hammersmith with me. I was working at the time, but I got a holiday booked as early as I possibly could. I said to my brother, 'I'm going to Spain.'

And he said, 'I want to come with you.'

But I said, 'No – you're too young.' He was too young – and Dickie Bird was too young, really. He asked me to swear to him that I wouldn't give him away. We travelled together and got to Paris. We went to the Communist Party office and they gave us a ticket for the Paris underground. As you go through, there's a list of stations, so we looked at the ticket we'd got, looked where the station was and what platform. When we got to the other end we were told, 'When you go outside the station, look across to your left and there's a café on a corner. Go in there, and don't talk to anybody on the ground floor. Go straight up the stairs – and there's a bloke up there.'

I think he spoke about six languages. He said, 'There's no need to ask you what language to speak to you, you're British – and you look like it.'

They got us to a safe house by taxi and we were there for several days. Then, by Tuesday, we were illegal. In those days you could go to Paris without a passport for a few days, but then you became illegal. One night a single-decker bus pulled up outside and there was a bloke with a list of names. My name was called but Dickie Bird's wasn't. I didn't want to say, 'No, I can't come' because they'd think I was backing out. But at least Dickie was with good friends, people we'd met there. So I said I'd see him when he got through – but unfortunately I never saw him again.

The coach took us to a farmhouse where we were fed, then the bus took us on to the foothills of the Pyrenees, near Perpignan. We went out into the country, so we could stop where there were no lights. The driver pulled up and said over his loudspeaker, 'I want all of you to get out and lie down on the floor. Once I put my lights on you'll be visible – so get down on the floor. I can't move without lights.' So he drove off and a bloke comes down the mountainside and he's got lots of rope-soled canvas shoes tied round his neck. Of course he didn't have my size – I took a size thirteen – so he had nothing to fit me. I had to go on with my civvy shoes, but being proper shoes they had leather soles and were slippery. I was hanging onto the stones. All the same, I got over the top all right, and we eventually reached some sort of fort at Figueres. From there we were taken on lorries to a station.

From the station we went to Albacete, where we signed on, then we were sent to a little town in the countryside near Madrid. We were under a bloke who had been in the IRA –

and he was good, a nice bloke. We had to do all our training with wooden cut-outs – the only gun we had that you could use was a light machine gun, bought from Mexico.

After drilling, they took the wooden cut-outs away and gave you a rifle as you stepped into the front line at Jarama. I got my rifle and was sent to a very deep trench along with Esmond Romilly, one of Churchill's nephews. The trench had a seat cut out up at the top and there were sandbags. I was told to sit up there and keep watch, and, if I saw a movement, to shoot. But I wasn't to waste ammunition. I saw movement, so I pressed the trigger – and I was on the floor! Romilly said, 'Is that the first time you've fired one?'

I said, 'Yes.'

He said, 'Get up there quickly and fire again – or you'll never fire one again. This time, pull the gun back into your shoulder – you didn't do that.' He told me it was the recoil of the rifle that had knocked me off my seat.

I was in the trenches being fired at every day. The Fascists would try to drop mortars into the trench – and they managed it a couple of times and blokes got wounded. After six weeks we went out on rest. We were camping out in a churchyard and I was laughing and talking with the blokes, then we put our groundsheets down between the gravestones and went to sleep. In the morning I couldn't get up. I could not raise my head. I called one of the blokes to pull me up, and he helped me to my feet but I couldn't walk. I had to crawl to the door of the sickbay – which was just a room with four beds in it. The one in charge was a Boots chemist, and he put me to bed.

Later he was sitting down at his table having his lunch and he looked across at me. I was getting a bit fidgety and I heard him say, 'I don't like the looks of that bloke.' He covered his lunch up, came over and stuck a thermometer in my mouth. Then he went running! Called the doctor, who was an International Brigader, then he called a more senior doctor from the Spanish army. This one said, 'Madrid!' and they had to get an ambulance to take me from this town to the hospital for infectious diseases in Madrid.

They thought it was typhoid, although I found out later that it was colitis. Colitis and typhoid are the same bug, but typhoid is when it attacks the stomach and colitis is when it attacks the colon. The ambulance driver was American and drove like a madman; as I looked out the trees flashed past like a fence. When we got there they put me on a flat trolley and wheeled me into the hospital and straight into bed. But the Spanish people in those days were a short race – not many tall ones – so when I got into the bed my feet were sticking out the bottom between the rails. One of the nurses went and got a chair and a pillow and rested my feet up. I was the first 'International' in there. The other boys were nearly all young Spanish soldiers. They used to laugh at me because I didn't know a word of Spanish then. I hadn't had a chance to learn.

The nurse told me that there was another nurse working upstairs who had been working in the Fulham hospital during the First World War. She spoke English, and they said she'd be glad to come downstairs and talk to me to help her remember her English. She came down every afternoon and sat and talked to me. She was very good – she taught me some Spanish, like how to count up to twenty. Then she taught me how to say 'Good morning' and 'Good afternoon'. I found out how to tell girls how lovely they were, and she was quite clever and very helpful to me. When I came out of the hospital I could at least speak to the Spanish people. A little boy came up to me and said, 'Americano, eh? Me speak English.' Then he said something else to me – and it was a swear word.

So I said, 'Come over here', and we sat down. I said, 'In English you say, "Hello – good morning" or "Good afternoon". I can tell you what you said to me in your own language', and I told him.

The poor little fellow – he was shocked. So I said, 'Don't worry, lad, it's not your fault. It's the stupid man who told you that was English.'

When I got out of the hospital my lot – the 15th Brigade – was at Brunete, so I got a lift there on a truck. I met up with a couple of blokes there, and a Hungarian doctor, who said to me, 'I need another stretcher-bearer.' The bloke who was on the back end of the stretcher came up to me, and, although he was a tall bloke, he was not quite as tall as me, so I ended up taking the front.

We crossed the Ebro. It was a big, fast-flowing river and they had a thick wire hawser strung right across it, with a deep metal barge hanging on it. Once you got in the barge, you pulled a rope that went round a pulley and you hauled yourself across. When you got out, they pulled it back and another crowd got in. We were being strafed and dive-bombed all the time, but our group was lucky and got through without a casualty. On the other side it was all open warfare. We were into action almost immediately – luckily by this time we had proper rifles.

There was a plateau on top of the hill, and the Fascists were on the other side of it. Then somebody was injured but they didn't call us stretcher-bearers; the bloke's mate just went out and got him, and he got a bullet through the thigh. They treated him locally, but they put the other wounded man on our stretcher and we carried him from there until we found an ambulance station. We got him on the ambulance and then came back. While we were carrying him, I had felt a draught go past my ear – a bullet. I could hear it and felt the draught, and I reckon it was a sniper in the trees. I looked round and couldn't see anybody – otherwise I would have fired back.

As soon as we got back there was another boy injured – this time down in the valley. So we ran back down the hill – I was on the front of the stretcher as usual – and we heard some men laughing. They later swore that my mate at the back of the stretcher didn't touch the ground. But the enemy on the other side had a heavy machine gun and the bullets were zipping just in front of my feet as I was running. You could see them going into the ground. He couldn't have been a very well-trained marksman, because he was following me down, and I got to the bottom without being hit. If he'd stopped lowering his gun, I'd have run into it – I couldn't have done anything else.

When we reached the boy he said to me, 'I've lost me razor.' I said, 'Bugger your razor, mate, you can buy another one of those, but you can't buy another you. Those bullets are just missing you.' We dragged him away – he'd got a very severe wound to his left knee, so we lifted him very gently onto the stretcher, put a field dressing on it and started to carry him out. He was a heavy bloke and I said, 'There's no way we're going to climb that hill. We'll go round it.' So we went round it.

My mate said to me, 'You've got the heavy end – you must be getting tired.' He said we should change over for a while, so I went to the back.

But when we lifted the bloke up, he screamed – he couldn't stand the pain – so we put him down again, and I said to my mate, 'You go back again to the back, and I'll manage the front all right.' It was the change of elevation that was causing the pain. Eventually we got him to the ambulance.

I saw that lad again in London after the war. Our first reunion was at Earl's Court and Paul Robeson was speaking and singing. This bloke came up to me – he was on crutches as he'd lost his leg from the knee down – and he said, 'I've come to say thank you, Lofty, for carrying me all that way.'

I said, 'It doesn't seem to have done you any good, mate.'

But he said, 'I'll get over it.'

After that we were posted on what they called Hill 666 – holding that – and I was back on the rifle. I killed one of them . . . Right below my position there was a lot of greenery, and suddenly three of the enemy came out from behind a little hillock and walked towards the cover of the greenery. Each one was carrying a shell. There was a hidden storage chest that they'd stored the shells in, and now they had one each. I tried to judge the distance – I thought it was around six hundred yards. There was a little sight on our rifles to help get the distance so I set it at six and got it loaded ready. When they came out and were walking across this open ground, I let fly with it. The first one nearest to me went down and never moved – never moved. They came out that night to take him. I know I got one back for one of our boys.

Eventually we were relieved from 666, and then we were in open warfare most of the time, fighting from village to village. We thought we were attacking – but we weren't making much ground. We didn't know it, but we were going forwards and back. It was bloody hard work, but we felt we were winning at the time.

After that I was put on kitchen duty – and had an accident. I had a great big fire burning and a cauldron of rice on it – I had to keep it stirring because it was the only food we'd got for the battalion that night. I was wearing puttees, and they were all frayed down the edges. The wind changed and I was standing close to windward. The flames caught all the frayed edges and burnt me pretty badly. I called out for one of the blokes to come over and I told him what to do to keep the rice stirred. Then I took the burnt puttees off and went up to the sickbay. The doctor put a bandage on it, but it turned septic. I was in agony and was whisked off to the hospital and was there for quite a long time.

Later on it got worse again and I had to go back to hospital, this time in a small town near Alicante, on the coast. I said to the doctor, 'I'm fed up with sitting around. I didn't come out to have a holiday – I came out to help the Spanish people, not be a drain on them. Can't you find me work?'

He said, 'Go and find my woman.' I knew who he meant because the matron of the hospital was his wife.

I went to see her and she taught me how to cut gauze so there were no rough edges showing, and swabs for cleaning wounds. We filled this big jar up and she stuck it in the sterilising machine. Then I went on re-rolling bandages that had been boiled, so they could be used again. Then I went through to help the doctor, and he'd got people coming in with new wounds. I was sitting by him and there was this great big jar with long forceps to take them out, and he said in his broken English, 'You put your fingers in that jar and I'll kick your arse all the way out of the hospital.' You had to take them out with the sterilised forceps and you put them in the sterilising liquid again.

I helped him with the wounds, and even a couple of operations. The first one he wanted the bloke held down, because he told me he'd only got this flat-topped table – no straps on it, nothing. He said the only anaesthetic he'd got was ether. The person being operated on would not feel the knife, he said, but, because it was ether, it doesn't stop the nerves, and the nerves react. He said, 'They jump – and that's why we have to strap them down. You're a big, strong bloke. I want you to hold this man down.'

They laid him down on the table and I saw he'd had a bullet go through his shoulder, which had taken a piece of shirt and a piece of jacket in with it. The doctor got this long-handled instrument with a tiny ball on the bottom of it – it looked like silver, but it was sterilised. He probed around and then he pulled out the jacket and the shirt, and then I could hear him touching the bullet – and eventually he brought that out, too. He used scissors to enlarge the hole so he could get the instruments in and when he did that I had to fight to keep my stomach from erupting. I hated the sound of it – but after that, whenever he wanted help, I was willing to do it.

One day they sent the planes over this little town. We couldn't understand why because there wasn't any military stuff there – just our little hospital. But they bombed the town and a number of the local people were wounded. They were all brought into the hospital. The doctor said to me, 'You can do that one – and you can do that one.' They were jobs he'd taught me to do. Then there was a lady who had a wound in a very embarrassing position, and she didn't want me to treat her, being a young bloke. She thought I shouldn't do it, but still I said to the doctor, 'There are jobs there I can't do – so you've got to do them – but this I can do.' She must have understood somehow, because she let me treat the wound and put the bandage on. I had to bandage all round the body to hold it. I managed it without touching her. I was pretty good at bandaging. She came through all right. There were a lot of people from the town and we treated them all – just the two of us. No nurses – just the doctor and me. The doctor was Jan Kisling, I think.

I was in that hospital about six weeks while my leg was being treated. I still have pain in it, naturally. To treat it they had cut up strips of gauze and soak them in spirit. When they put it on it was ice-cold until they got the bandage on – and then it was like being on fire. It was very painful. I couldn't lie down and read or anything like that. I used to walk around the hospital and look out of the windows. The main thing was to keep busy and do something – I'd gone there to help, after all.

I came home from there for Christmas 1938. They put a dressing on my leg, like a cast – rubberised – to stop me scratching. I was loaded onto a train that had to stop several times in tunnels because we were being bombed. Eventually we got to the border station, then went through onto the boat. There was no trouble at the border because by then it was all over. There was one bloke – a Welsh miner with a red head, who we used to call Ginger – like I was always called Gibbo. Well, on the way out of the French port the sea was so rough that the ship bumped into the harbour wall. The captain gave out over the loudspeaker that nobody was allowed outside except the sailors – and they had to be on a safety rope. That was how rough it was. As we were coming out, the boat was lurching up and down and Ginger was terribly seasick. There was all this lovely food laid out in the dining room, but he couldn't face it. I remember him mumbling, 'Why don't they dig that bleeding tunnel?'

Back in England, my mum and one of my brothers were on Victoria Station and so pleased to see me. My youngest brother was a barber and he'd got several straight razors, so he cut this cast off my leg. When my father saw the wound, he said, 'Christ, you won't work for another five weeks.' But I said I'd start work tomorrow if he had work for me. I went to my doctor – an Irishman – who was very good indeed. He knew where I'd been, because he was a bit left wing himself. He cleaned up the wound and said he'd clear it up for me. I asked him when could I start work, and he told me the sooner the better.

He said, 'I don't mind if you could go to work tomorrow – the more you work on that, the more it will keep the blood flowing and keep it healing. It will be painful but it will be worth it.' So I worked for a few months, then the pain got the better of me, so I started looking for a job without so much work up and down stairs. I'd done cooking, so I went and got a job as a chef in a gentlemen's club just round the corner from the American Embassy. It was in Grosvenor Street, at the 66 Club, and I was there for over two years and did two Christmases.

Dickie Bird got wounded at Brunete – a burst of machine-gun fire – and he didn't survive. I don't even know where he's buried, but his name is on the plaque in Bishop's Park. I made sure they put his name down, and I was there when it was unveiled. I had some good mates out there. When you travel such a lot with different units you get to know people – some of the finest blokes I've ever met were there, and that includes Churchill's nephew, Esmond Romilly.

I'd do it all again – Spain. And if I could meet that bugger Franco, I'd shoot him. I was terribly upset when the Republic lost. There were people I knew who couldn't have got away. They must have been captured and shot. That made me feel that I'd run away – but I hadn't. I'd stayed to the end. I did my best. And I'd do the same again.

PADDY COCHRANE

Born 11 March 1913 in Dublin

I was born and schooled in Dublin, and I got my left-wing leanings very early on from my father, who was a strong Socialist. When I was just a young boy of seven, my father was taken out into the garden by the Black and Tans and shot. They left him for dead – but he wasn't. I was there when they came but it seems I was asleep, so they tried to open my eyes to see if I was feigning. They left a glass pistol full of whisky for the house when they went – but Father was already wounded.

I remember losing my father. I was in the same bedroom as he was and I remember him saying to me, looking across the road to the hospital opposite, 'Look at the way they've painted that door blue' – and it was white. He was raving a bit, and he died two or three months after that.

When my father died we were still living in Eccles Street in

Dublin, opposite the Mater Hospital, but the house was lease-hold. When the lease ended, my mother asked the eldest of my three uncles, Uncle Arthur, about paying the lease. He did, and the next uncle, Sid, did, too, but the third uncle wouldn't pay, with the result that we lost the house. It was terrible for the family. All my sisters were sent away and one of them I never saw again.

Also living in Eccles Street was a woman called Madame Charlotte Despard and her friend, Madame Constance Markievicz, who was a very active suffragette. I remember so well the local parish priest, leading groups of drunkards – because that's what they were. These men went to Mass in the morning, but they didn't even go into the church – they stayed out in the doorway, so that they could say they'd been to Mass, then they all marched up the street to Madame Despard's house.

There was always tremendous oratory going on at the bottom of Findlaters Hill in Dublin, and I used to go along listen to Maud Gonne, the Irish Nationalist, and Charlotte Despard, who often spoke there. There was always somebody speaking – left wing, right wing, middling or whatever – or a priest. Always somebody with something to say.

When I'd just turned fourteen I'd left school and was working in a little automobile place. It was a small branch of the Reliance Bearing and Gear Company in Cork and they had a little office in Dublin. The garage was next door to a pub in Eustace Street, and the manager used to come in, read the post then go straight into the pub and stay there all day long. He'd be absolutely sozzled – so he left the running of the company to me, just a boy. While I was there, a man came from America – a Mr Sternard – to sell spare parts for Fords to the company. We were talking together – while my boss was absolutely up to his eyes in beer and whisky next door – and I asked him if there was any chance of me having a job with him in America – and he said 'Yes'.

That was July, and by September I was in America. I had a job straight away – and I stayed in that job for a year. Then I thought I'd have a go exploring and I went north. I should have gone south but I ended up in Alaska, and that was in May. The snow was up to the tops of the houses on all sides of the road. How they kept the roads clear I don't know – you have a couple of inches of snow here now and there's chaos. I didn't like the frost at all and I hitch-hiked down the west coast of Canada, right to the bottom and across to Three Rivers, and from there I booked a passage back to Liverpool.

I was twenty-three, still in Liverpool, and looking after myself, when the Spanish war broke out – and I wanted to go. I'd always had left-wing thoughts, and I wanted to go because I hated Mosley. He used to organise marches, and there was always trouble and fighting would break out. I got involved in the anti-Fascist movement – but not in the fights. They just broke out between people who wanted to fight, but I didn't.

I learnt about Spain from the *News Chronicle*, which I used to buy to look for a job. I felt it was my duty to go to Spain, not just because I was having a hell of a time getting a job.

Everywhere I went the notices said 'No Irish need apply', so I was barred from practically every job I went for. I left Liverpool and headed towards Birmingham – but still it was 'No Irish need apply'.

The *News Chronicle* was pro the Spanish Government – whereas most other papers were pro-Franco. I knew about Fascism – and how Fascists were threatening to come over to England and Ireland. I hated all dictators because of Hitler. What was amazing to me was that later Hitler successfully invaded France – but Franco didn't support him. I couldn't understand that, or, indeed why, after that, the Germans turned round and attacked Russia – which they did instead of coming to England. They would have had an easy job here, despite all the preparation and the Home Guard. But in 1936 we hated Franco – and Mussolini and Hitler.

I was very upset about the non-intervention agreement – very, very upset – because there were a great number of people who were marching in England for the right to support the Spanish Government – and they wouldn't let them. I went on those marches, too.

When the Spanish war started I really wanted to get to Spain, and be involved. My family didn't have any knowledge of my going – but I hitch-hiked down to London and went to the Communist headquarters. At first they wouldn't take me because I hadn't any military skills, but later they'd take you, whatever you were. I'd looked in the *News Chronicle* and there was a notice: 'Wanted – drivers to take ambulances out to Spain' – and keep them out there. When I first joined up, just off Oxford Street, I was given around two and six to get something to eat. I went into a café, ordered a dinner and when they put it in front of me I fainted from hunger. They took my dinner away and kept it warm and gave it back to me when I came to. I was OK then but it was a nasty old turn.

They were organising ambulances to go out to Spain – one was from the printers' union and others were paid for and donated by various other unions. I didn't belong to any union at that time. Nobody asked me to join – but I would have if they'd asked.

Luckily I'd learnt to drive in Dublin. There was a Scout movement I'd joined, and we used to go off to a little cul-de-sac with a garage at the top, and in there was a 1910 De Dion Bouton. We boys used to take turns to drive it down to the bottom of the street and back up again – and that's how I learnt to drive. I'd also ridden a motorbike – I had an old Francis Barnett with the triangular tank and triangulated frame. I taught myself to drive that – and a few other lads as well. I didn't have a licence then – there was no such thing – and I didn't get a licence until I came back to England and went to drive the ambulance to Spain. They gave me a licence then, but there was no test whatsoever.

Once I signed up, we were sent to the place where you go for sports clothes – it may have been Moss Bros – which had a number of branches across London. This one was in Oxford Street, and we were supplied with jackboots, knee breeches, a leather jacket and a peaked cap. That was a sort of uniform for the ambulance people then.

There were six ambulances sent out and I took one of them, along with a co-driver. We picked up the ambulance in London and drove to Newhaven, crossed to Dieppe, then drove all the way down through the middle of France to Perpignan. From there we drove across the Pyrenees and into Spain. There was a little Dublin man, who had money from the Spanish Aid people to buy us oil and petrol and pay for our hotels as well. He paid for everything. There was also a little crippled man who was a fluent French speaker, and he used to interpret for us on the way down.

My co-driver was a funny lad – but he was all right – but suddenly, when we got to Spain, there was not a sign of him. I think he was captured. As we drove through, we had a load of bars of Cadbury's chocolate in the compartment under the seat – it had all been donated to the cause – and the kids in Spain would all gather around us when we stopped, and I handed out bars of chocolate to them.

Once in Spain we headed to Barcelona, where we were still looked after by the Irishman who held the money for the trip. There was a flat there which was used by transient people who were going to fight for the Government side. Once I got to meet them, I thought the Spanish people were very nice. They were much, much nicer than the French. They were very friendly and they would take you into their houses and give you coffee or a *café con leche* – which was a glass of milk with a dash of coffee in it.

We were allocated our various jobs. I thought I was going to drive an ambulance in Spain – but I only did this for a short while. I remember one of my first jobs was to pick up some sick Spanish soldiers from the front line. When I arrived there were twelve altogether – six with syphilis and five with gonorrhoea and one other to take to the hospital!

One day, like a stupid bugger, I drove the ambulance down to the border on the river and crossed the Armanda Bridge straight into Fascist territory. Like a fool I drove across in the ambulance and all the enemy machine guns went off with bullets ripping through the top of the ambulance. The bullets missed me, but you've never seen a three-point turn done as quick in your life! It was one of the most stupid things I ever did.

I'd been in Spain about six weeks when I switched from the ambulance to driving a lorry, because I felt that I was doing a better job, carting big loads about during the lulls as well as transporting quite a few wounded soldiers – the walking wounded. We used to move hospitals as well, and carry all the beds from one place to another. That was the first time, apart from my father being shot, that I saw badly injured people. I worked with Reggie Saxon for a while – he was the first man to introduce anaesthetics out there.

I saw my first action when I was driving a truck – I was carrying things backwards from the lines and a chap held me up and commandeered the truck. He was the captain of two anti-tank guns and he loaded them onto my truck and off we all went.

On another occasion we were moving a whole hospital – and we sat down for a rest by the side of this narrow road next to a field. I was sitting there and I'd just said, 'Oh, blimey, I'm tired' and, whish, a bullet went right in between my legs and hit the floor – a very near thing indeed. I wondered what was protecting me then.

The Fascists were holding the town of Belchite, and we moved forwards to take it. I drove there in the truck and went to the top of the street. I looked down on it and I saw these two trucks in the square. There was a lull – I didn't know there was any fighting, I didn't even know that the Fascists held the place. I thought it was ours, and that's why I ventured to the top of the street. When I saw these two trucks, I thought I'd go down with my partner and hot-wire them to start them. I was starting to walk, when a hand grenade came and hit the floor by my feet.

I tried to turn myself around, away from it, but it hit the ground as I turned, and I got the detonator in there and out between my bum and got all this shrapnel in my back and shoulder and wrist. I don't know what I thought at the time, but I crawled into a house in the road parallel to the main street, on the hill, which was, I suppose, ten to fifteen yards from the top.

I was losing a lot of blood from little wounds, and a lot from my leg, so I sat on my leg to stop the bleeding – I had quite a lot of medical first-aid training in the ambulances – and I sat on it through the night. In the dark I could hear something moving, and that worried me, but when dawn came I looked up and there was a bloody old goat. I'd thought it was a man.

It felt like a very long night; all I know is that I dozed for a while, because you sleep at night, no matter how hurt you are. There was no sound of fighting going on around the area at all. It had stopped. The next morning a man turned up – I thought he was Canadian, but he was an American – and he came in shouting 'Any Americans down here?'

I said, 'No, but there's an Irishman!' and he came in and he carried me out, under fire, up to the top of the hill.

I've tried hard since to find him, but I've never been able to. I suppose he must be dead. He'd come back and I think it was only for me. I think of my stupidity in walking down there, but, once I was wounded, I had to find somewhere to go with my leg bleeding so much.

The American took me up to the road, put me down, and then went to see if there were any more in that house. He came back then carried me to a truck and took me back to the hospital. I was in the hospital for a short while, and I remember an Irishman in the bed opposite me dying of his wounds – somehow or other you get blasé about these things. When there's so much death around you, you take it for granted – as a regular thing.

I always felt it was worthwhile – I never felt 'silly bugger'. I always felt very serious about it and there were so many people who were of the same mind as myself. I got visitors in the hospital – one was a great friend of mine, Max Cohen, and he unfortunately was hit by a hand grenade as well, but he didn't survive it. I was bloody lucky really, because mine was quite a serious wound. I was three weeks in the hospital in Spain, and then they sent me back to London. There was somebody going back with a van and he took me with him. We drove all the way to the French border and, because my passport wasn't signed, they wanted to put me in jail until they'd sorted it out. This lad was a civilian – not a military man – and I don't know what he was doing in Spain; he might have been on a newspaper. Anyway, he got me through the border and we came back to London.

I was handed over to someone in the hospital in Stonebridge, in northwest London, who fortunately was a sympathiser of the Spanish war. My wounds at this stage were bandaged and not giving much trouble, except there was still shrapnel in them, so this nurse took the pieces out. She was taking bits of shrapnel out of me and dropping them in a bowl and saying, 'There you are, look at that.'

I said, 'Is that all?'

She replied 'Why, isn't it enough?'

I didn't return to Spain, and I missed my friends – I didn't have an address to write to them but I was pretty woozy in any case. But I didn't feel left out of it because I was very, very kindly treated by the people in Stonebridge.

In October 1938 I heard that the Brigaders were leaving Spain, and I was amazed. I went down to the station to meet them on their way back but I mistook the day. I sat there and waited for them for a long time. Later there were a lot of marches through London, and Brigaders were always at the head of some left-wing movement or Labour Party march – and I felt proud to belong to them. I still feel very proud to have been to Spain. I don't really know if there's a lesson to be learnt from it – the government played ball with Franco for a while, and one way and another they kept themselves out of trouble.

You always expected your side to win. You always expected that. But that time we didn't – we weren't strong enough and were too disunited.

I'm beginning to feel old but it's really only this year – it's my hearing! I think it was the anti-tank guns that did it, you know. Because I spent quite a little while on the anti-tank guns in Spain, and they were noisy buggers. The CRACK of them. They weren't a bang, they were a crack – and I think that's what has caused my deafness.

We went and, yes, I would do it all over again – I would if I was healthy. I've done nothing that I'm ashamed of and I've done nothing I'm concerned about. I think I've lived quite a good life. I've lived very happily here – while my wife was alive we were all right.

TIMELINE OF THE SPANISH CIVIL WAR

1930

28 January   Spanish dictator Miguel Primo de Rivera is
                forced to resign.

1931

14 April   King Alfonso XIII flees the country as the
                Second Spanish Republic is declared. The
                elected Republican-Socialist government
                embarks on a programme of social reforms
                to improve conditions for the impoverished
                working classes.

1933

19 November   A coalition of right-wing parties, including
                the Catholic CEDA party, wins election over

the divided left and starts to overturn the previous government's reforms.

1934

6 October   Spain's President proclaims martial law throughout Spain and the president of the Generalidad declares Cataluña a fully independent republic. Government troops immediately move in to squash the separatist movement – Catalan autonomy is voided and Madrid regains control.

1935

September   POUM, the Workers Party of Marxist Unification is formed by Andres Nin and Joaquin Maurin.

1936

11 January   The Socialist and Communist parties sign an electoral pact.

15 January   The Spanish Popular Front is orchestrated by and organised under former Republican prime minister, Manuel Azaña.

16 February   The Popular Front wins the general election.

10 May   Azaña becomes President of the Spanish Republic.

18 July   A military uprising on the Spanish mainland is the start of the civil war.

	General Franco stages successful military uprisings in Morocco and issues a manifesto.
24 July	Franco's rebel forces capture Granada.
26 July	Hitler pledges military aid to support the Fascist rebellion.
4 August	Franco leads the Nationalist Army to capture Badajoz on the way to Madrid.
8 August	France closes her border and prevents volunteers from crossing into Spain.
12 August	The first volunteers for the International Brigades arrive in Spain.
15 August	British Prime Minister Stanley Baldwin announces a ban on the export of arms to Spain.
28 August	Franco's Nationalist Army bombs Madrid.
9 September	Twenty-seven countries form a non-intervention committee in London.
21 September	The Nationalists announce General Franco as head of state.
27 September	The march on Madrid is delayed while Franco's forces relieve the siege of the Alcázar in Toledo.
1 October	Franco is invested as Chief of the Spanish State.
12 October	The Spanish Republic receives its first aid shipment from the Soviet Union.
2 November	Nationalist troops take Brunete.

6 November	Nationalists start to besiege Madrid, forcing the Republican Government to move to Valencia.
18 November	Mussolini and Hitler recognise Franco's Fascist regime.
23 November	Franco abandons his attack on Madrid.

1937

6 January	America bans the export of arms to Spain.
8 February	Nationalist troops capture Malaga.
12 February	International Brigades halt the Nationalist Army at the Battle of Jarama.
26 April	The German Condor Legion carries out a devastating air attack on Guernica, the Basque capital in northern Spain.
10 May	A Nationalist uprising in Barcelona is put down by Republican troops.
19 June	Nationalist troops capture Bilbao.
26 June	Nationalists take Santander.
6 July	Republican troops under General Rojo launch an attack on Brunete.
28 August	The Vatican recognises Franco's regime.
1 October	Republican forces capture Belchite.
28 October	The Republican Government moves from Valencia to Barcelona.
8 December	Barcelona is bombed by Nationalist aircraft.
14 December	Republican troops open an offensive at Aragón.

1938

7 January	Republican troops take back the city of Teruel from Nationalist control.
22 February	Nationalists retake Teruel.
28 March	The Republican Minister for War calls for the start of peace negotiations.
15 April	Nationalists take the town of Vinaròs.
25 July	80,000 Republican troops start to advance across the River Ebro.
3 September	Nationalist forces break through the Republican lines at Gandesa.
21 September	Plans to withdraw International Brigades from Spain are announced.
4 October	All non-Spanish fighting in the Republican Army are withdrawn from the front line.
28 October	International Brigades farewell parade through the streets of Barcelona.
16 November	Republican troops defeated by Nationalists at River Ebro.

1939

25 January	With the city under threat, the Republican Government decamps from Barcelona to Figueres.
26 January	Nationalist troops take Barcelona.
4 February	Azaña flees across the French border.
27 February	British Prime Minister Neville Chamberlain recognises Franco's regime.

4 March	Juan Negrín attempts to form a Communist government for such land as the Republicans still control.
27 March	After a siege of nearly three years, the Nationalist Army finally enters Madrid.
30 March	Valencia is taken by Franco's troops.
1 April	Franco announces the end of the civil war.

La Pasionaria's (communist deputy, Dolores Ibárruri) farewell speech to the International Brigades, at a parade at which more than 300,000 lined the streets.

BARCELONA, 28 OCTOBER 1938

It is very difficult to say a few words in farewell to the heroes of the International Brigades, because of what they are and what they represent. A feeling of sorrow, an infinite grief catches our throat: *sorrow* for those who are going away, for the soldiers of the highest ideal of human redemption, exiles from their countries, persecuted by the tyrants of all peoples; *grief* for those who will stay here forever mingled with the Spanish soil, in the very depth of our heart, hallowed by our feeling of eternal gratitude.

From all peoples, from all races, you came to us like brothers, like sons of immortal Spain; and, in the hardest days of the war, when the capital of the Spanish Republic was threatened, it was you, gallant comrades of the International Brigades, who helped save the city with your fighting enthusiasm, your heroism and your spirit of sacrifice. And Jarama and Guadalajara, Brunete and Belchite, Levante and the Ebro, in immortal verses sing of the courage, the sacrifice, the daring, the discipline of the men of the International Brigades.

For the first time in the history of the peoples' struggles, there was the spectacle, breathtaking in its grandeur, of the formation of International Brigades to help save a threatened country's freedom and independence – the freedom and independence of our Spanish land.

Communists, Socialists, Anarchists, Republicans – men of different colours, differing ideology, antagonistic religions – yet all profoundly loving liberty and justice, they came and offered themselves to us unconditionally.

They gave us everything – their youth or their maturity; their science or their experience; their blood and their lives; their hopes and aspirations – and they asked us for nothing. But, yes, it must be said, they did want a post in battle, they aspired to the honour of dying for us.

Banners of Spain! *Salute* these many heroes! Be *lowered* to honour so many martyrs!

Mothers! Women! When the years pass by and the wounds of war are staunched, when the memory of the sad and bloody days dissipates in a present liberty, of peace and well-being, when the rancours have died out and pride in a free country is felt equally by all Spaniards, *speak to your children.* Tell them of the men of the International Brigades.

Recount for them how, coming over seas and mountains, crossing frontiers bristling with bayonets, sought by raving dogs thirsting to tear their flesh, these men reached our country as crusaders for freedom, to fight and die for Spain's liberty and independence, threatened by German and Italian Fascism. They gave up everything – their loves, their countries, home and fortune, fathers, mothers, wives, brothers, sisters and children – and they came and said to us: 'We are here. Your cause, Spain's cause, is ours. It is the cause of all advanced and progressive mankind.'

Today many are *departing*. Thousands *remain*, shrouded in Spanish earth, profoundly remembered by all Spaniards. Comrades of the International Brigades: political reasons, reasons of state, the welfare of that very cause for which you offered your blood with boundless generosity, are sending you back, some to your own countries and others to forced exile. You can go proudly. You are history. You are legend. You are the heroic example of democracy's solidarity and universality in the face of the vile and accommodating spirit of those who interpret democratic principles with their eyes on hoards of wealth or corporate shares which they want to safeguard from all risk.

We shall not forget you; and, when the olive tree of peace is in flower, entwined with the victory laurels of the Republic of Spain – return!

Return to our side for here you will find a homeland – those who have no country or friends, who must live deprived of friendship; all, all will have the affection and gratitude of the Spanish people who today and tomorrow will shout with enthusiasm –

Long live the heroes of the International Brigades!

INDEX

Subheadings are shown in
approximate chronological order
where appropriate.

PICTURE CREDITS

Page 1: Lou Kenton – Mark Read; Page 2: Penny Feiwel – Sam Frost;
Page 3: Jack Jones – Eamonn McCabe; Page 4: Jack Edwards – Mark Read;
Page 5: Bob Doyle – Mark Read; Page 6: Sam Lesser – Eamonn McCabe;
Page 7: Les Gibson – Echo Newspapers; Page 8: Paddy Cochrane –
Christopher Thomond/Guardian News & Media Ltd 2008